Gee You Are You

Gee You Are You

Krishna Prem (Michael Mogul)

Library of Congress Cataloging-in-Publication Data

Printed in the United States of America

First Printing: July, 2011

ISBN-978-1-61364-318-1

About the Author

Gee You Are You is a book about life's journey from 'here to here.' On the front cover is a picture of me at 33 years of age, sitting on a cold marble floor in front of my teacher and friend, Osho, in Pune, India. On the back cover I am the ripe old age of 66. As Bob Dylan once sang, "Oh, but I was so much older then, I'm younger than that now." Yes my body is now twice as old and yet I feel half my age... the magic of meditation. Through my years of peeling the layers of my own onion, I have turned my life from maditation in the world to meditation in my inner world. When reading this book, you will be constantly challenged to witness that you are not so much your conditioning in the marketplace of your home town, but more that the world is appearing in you... that you are not the mind. And more than that you are a child of the universe who is in charge of his own existence. In meditation this is often called No-Mind. So get ready to know just how big you are... that your mind is no longer your boss. Love is, Krishna Prem.

Contents

Note: Chapter Titles are the names of Osho Books that I have
loved, especially Tantra: The Supreme Understanding And
Ecstasy: The Forgotten Language.

Go to www.osho.com for further information.

Prologue

"This is the time for everybody to meditate. This is the time that, except for meditation, nothing can help you to get out of your misery. And meditation is a simple phenomenon. Just whenever you have time, sit silently, doing nothing. Relax, close your eyes, watch your thoughts as if you are watching a movie on the screen. You are just a watcher. If you can watch your thoughts just as if they are moving there on the screen, and you are not involved in them, they start dispersing. It is your involvement that gives them life energy. When you withdraw yourself and become just a witness, thoughts start falling, like leaves which are dead start falling from the trees. Soon you will be surprised, the screen is empty. Consciousness coming back to the original source is what I call enlightenment. This blissfulness happens here and now."
The Last Testament, Vol 5, Osho

Sitting together with Osho in '74 in his Woodlands apartment in Bombay on our one-year anniversary, I asked him how it is that he reads me like an open book. He smiled as he hinted that when he found out who he is, he also met me and that in reality we are not two. Almost giggling by now, he said that we are both buddhas, that he is a waking buddha and I am a sleeping buddha. "Not much difference, eh?" No one had ever called me a buddha before, so that felt fine, but a sleeping buddha…my young spiritual ego took a hit. Osho asked me how my meditation was coming along. He had asked me to do the Dynamic Meditation for twenty-one mornings before our meeting. What rolled off my lips is what Groucho Marx famously said, "Close, but no cigar." Osho's giggle turned into a hearty laugh. I went on to explain that it was not so much as getting out of my mind, but it was more like I was moving furniture (thoughts) around in my home (mind).

He looked at me sternly as he said, "Do not decorate your prison."

I have come to know that our minds are prisons until we are free, until we can watch our minds work for us instead of the other way around. Until we become the witness. Becoming the witness is the key to unlocking the mystery of this little book. Quite simply the witness is who you are as you watch what you do and think and feel. The witness is who you are. To remember that you are the witness requires that you become intimate with yourself. You can no longer treat yourself like a perfect stranger...what you need now is love plus a touch of awareness. Please don't get depressed that you have wasted your entire life up to now. You can know. Your life is a journey and quite simply the journey is the goal. Trust yourself. The present is a present, so let's start now, and when I say you, I am talking to myself as well. I am you and you are me and we are all together. You will need to quiet your mind to witness yourself as your character (your personality) running around in circles chasing your tail. As the waking Buddha reminds, "Be still and know."

In the West, when I ask my friends, "Tell me who you are?" I often get an answer back, "I am a doctor, a lawyer, an Indian chief." I get the answer of the doer. In the East, I often hear the sound of silence to that exact same question...an answer from your very being.

The question is, when are we becoming human beings instead of human doers? A human being also is a human doer, but he moves from his center, always remaining a witness when he moves into the cyclone of the marketplace.

From this very moment go back into your prison, into your mind. Now open the windows and the doors and your skylight. Let misery blow through you. Don't grab onto it. Let bliss tickle you. This too will pass. Misery and bliss are both experiences. I wonder which experience you prefer. Do not choose. Life comes, life goes, and you are also not here to decorate your prison. Make a clean break. Freedom is the highest value, even higher than love. Freedom is you watching your mind without reacting. Freedom is responding to whatever life throws at you. In the East, this is known as No-Mind. In the West we doers call this the zone. In reality where there is no such thing as East or West, there is only life living, death dying while you remain the witness of this eternal play.

You are cordially invited to be a human being once and for all while your human doer gets involved in all sorts of dramas. You will know you are enlightened when your dramas unfold without touching you. For me right now the most important word in the English language is *and;* not Krishna Prem *or* you, but Krishna Prem *and* you. This book is not about meditating in the East or working downtown. It's about movement…moving from your center (your inner world) into the marketplace (your outer world) and back again. According to Osho, quite simply, "God is Movement."

Osho called this meeting of East and West Zorba the Buddha. You are aware of your Zorba. You know what it is to have fun in the world. Can you remain alert after one too many glasses of bubbly? At the same time, can you meditate while you sip? Again, for me, it's not Zorba *or* the Buddha, its Zorba *and* the Buddha. I'll drink to that if you are willing to close your eyes for twenty minutes and watch your breath before you dress for work today.

Yes, it is not your work to become someone in the future, but simply your play to remember who you are right now. Once and for all, life is not in your future, you are already alive and perfect. Wake up and disturb me. And I'll do the same for you.

Introduction

"Love.
You ask for my ten commandments. This is very difficult because
I am against any sort of commandment.
Yet just for the fun of it I set down what follows:

1. *Obey no orders except those from within.*
2. *The only God is life itself.*
3. *Truth is within, do not look for it elsewhere.*
4. *Love is prayer.*
5. *Emptiness is the door to truth, it is the means, the end*
   and the achievement.
6. *Life is here and now.*
7. *Live* fully *awake.*
8. *Do not swim, float.*
9. *Die each moment so that you are renewed each moment.*
10. *Stop seeking. That which is, is:* stop and see. *"*

A Cup of Tea, Osho

Thirty plus years ago I left America in search of myself and now I am on my way back home. It has taken me half my life to know that I am whole. My journey began in nineteen hundred and sixty something when I bought a one-way ticket to nowhere!

As the plane touched down in Bombay, India, I immediately had a feeling I can only describe as now-here. It was a feeling of coming home and it's no coincidence that India is called Mother

India. With my life savings of five hundred dollars in my pocket, and a warm feeling in my heart, I felt rich for the first time in my life.

So Marcia and I set off, hand in hand, on the Hippie Trail to the beaches of Goa. Marcia was the gal I had been traveling around planet Earth with for a while and was the love of my life at the time. We found our first honeymoon spot under a cashew tree, only a hundred yards of pure sand away from the Arabian Sea. However, our romantic relationship suffered its first hiccup just minutes after our first sip of the local H_2O. In Mexico they call it Montezuma's Revenge, in India they call it dysentery, but I just call it, plain and simple, the shits. Anyway, the shits soon turned our smooth-cruising relation-ship into a rocky "relation-shit!"

After our first mutual I-hate-your-guts fight, we turned our backs on each other and, lying yards apart on the beach, began reading our library books. Marcia picked up *Autobiography of a Yogi* by a fellow named Paramahansa Yogananda. I've never read it, and probably never will, as it must be a thousand pages long or so. Anyway, judging by the size of her book, I knew I would be living in the dog house for a while, rather than under that romantic cashew tree by the sea. I chose *Seeds of Revolutionary Thought,* a quick hundred-page read by Acharya Rajneesh, who later changed his name to Bhagwan Shree Rajneesh, and eventually to Osho.

Now, you may be thinking, "Oh no! Not *that* Bhagwan with the ninety-nine Rolls Royces? Can't stand him!" or you may be thinking, "Never heard of him." Either way, for me, Osho is the love of my life. You may not have a master or you may be in love with another master, but for me, Osho is the best-looking loving friend I have ever known, and all the other masters look like ugly ducklings. It's just like when you first fall in love, doesn't everybody else look ordinary to you? But Osho was quick to point out to me that Osho is the first and last Osho, that Jesus Christ is the first and last Christian, and it is my job to be the first and last Krishna Prem. And that brings me to the point; just as it's my job to be the first and last Krishna Prem: so it's your job to be the first and last YOU!

See, at the end of the day, it's not about the master at all, it's about you. The master isn't the place where you put down your bags; he's the signpost along the way, the finger pointing to the moon. It's about you becoming the master of your own reality. Ask yourself, who is the master of your life right now? Who is running the show? The answer is probably...your very own mind. And what I'm going to do in this book is help you understand the nature of your own mind, what it does, how it works and how its chattering thoughts are the ONLY obstacle to U knowing U.

It's no coincidence that G.U.R.U. has two U's in it! One U represents the little "u." That's the "u" that gets up in the morning, brushes its teeth, gets dressed, goes out and struts its stuff. It's your little local life; you can call it your "self," your

"I" or your "me." Then there's the other U, which is your big "U." That's the U who exists beyond your body, your mind and the entire world itself. It's the ultimate U, call it God, Source, Existence; call it what you like.

And that's my job here in this book, to help your little u get in touch with your big U, so you know who U are in total, and that there's no separation between the two! See, it's no good me knowing you are you, or others knowing you are you, no, that's not enough. *You* need to know *you are you*, and you have every right not to be satisfied until you do! Only when you know the cosmic joke, that *you are already you...* will you know that the world is a play, u are an actor and that life is not awful, but full of awe!

So, if you're ready, let's begin;

We're all searching for something whether it's Mr. or Mrs. Right, butt-loads of cash, the hottest wheels on the road, CEO status, supermodel legs or ultimate orgasm! We may be looking for the wildest, craziest, most happening party scene or just a simple, quiet life. Whether we know it or not, we're all chasing something. I mean, how many people do you know who can honestly say, "I don't want anything." Huh? Any? So, if we could boil down our search to just one word, what would it be? Love? Peace? Happiness? Security? Fulfillment? Perfection? Home? It?

And the strange thing is we all *know* there's something more, only we don't know quite what it is or quite where to look.

Some of us think we do know what we want, only to discover, once it lands on our doorstep, that that's not really it either. And, although we all seem to be following different goals and pursuits, we're ultimately all searching for that same mysterious, elusive thing, call it what you like. Only we're all searching in different ways, peeking round different corners and traveling at different speeds. Some of us are just casually wandering through life, turning over the odd stone every now and then to see what's underneath, while others of us are on a single-pointed mission, and are madly ripping the place apart, diving into every nook and cranny. I guess those of us who aren't really bothered will just take the slow boat to China, while those of us who are really desperate will leap onto the Orient Express. But either way, we're all searching for the answer to a question we don't even know.

Well, that question is, "Who am I?" and the answer is "You are already you!"

So why, you might ask, is there any point searching for something we already are? I mean, how dumb is that? And I would have to agree with you. Only just because we've read something is so, doesn't mean we *know* it is so, and there's a whole Kilimanjaro of difference in that! And why, we might also ask, is this searching business all so arduous and mysterious? Well actually it's not, it just appears that way. Paradoxically, coming to know U are U is the hardest yet simplest thing you will ever do. I guess it's like the long jump, the run-up itself takes a bit of effort, but once you're in the air it's pretty much plain sailing!

Ironically, the search only seems difficult because we're not used to doing simple things. Looking for who we are is like a fish in the ocean looking for water. It's like looking for our own eyes. It's like shining a lamp in a cave and looking for the light. It's there, right there, and we know it's there, only somehow we just can't find it. Why? Because we're wearing dark glasses, because we have a filter over our eyes which stops us from seeing clearly what's right under our nose, and this filter is our very own mind and our thinking. As long as we *think we know* who we are, we won't be able to recognize who we are.

Essentially, until we know who we are, we will continue searching. Until our belly is full, we will remain hungry. Until we have the answers to the questions, "What is life?" and, "What is death?" and, "Why on earth am I here?" we will keep questioning. Only when we are found, will the questions disappear and the answers with them. The fish in the sea is not thirsty and the real you is not hungry either.

Gee, you are you! Sounds very simple, sounds very cute… but what exactly does it mean? Well, it took me over sixty years to get to this very moment where I can say it means, "You are already you!" You are already it, you are already enough. There's nowhere to go, nothing to do and no one to become. You are already absolutely perfect and complete as you are; only you don't know it yet.

See, the good news is that coming to know U is not about creating, building or becoming someone new. It's not about changing, improving or healing yourself. You don't need to trade in the old U for a new U, because you're not this U OR that U, you're both U AND U. All you need to do is open your eyes and wake up to the true U. In fact, the journey home is not about doing anything; it is about *un*doing everything you've already done. It's about getting off the train of thinking, trying and becoming, dropping all your mental baggage, stripping off all those layers of ideas that aren't really you, and finally getting naked.

And, the really great thing is that when you know who you are, you know who everyone else is too. When you see your own hot buttons, you see everyone else's too. Then you know that there is no problem I have that you don't have too. Sure, we're all unique, with different main frames, CPU's and different wiring, so to speak, but fundamentally we're all the same machine. So if I'm already me, then you must be already you!

"Gee you are you" in American spells G.U.R.U! What can I say? That's what we Americans do; we shorten everything and speed everything up! I call it fast-food writing. G.U.R.U. is to me what BFF is to Paris Hilton; G.U.R.U. is a Best Friend Forever. But anyway, we've all heard the word and bought the T-shirt, but what exactly is a guru?

The dictionary says it's a religious or spiritual leader or teacher. That's cool, only I like to think of a guru as any teacher or guide, anyone we meet on our life journey, since everyone and everything is spiritual anyway. Parents are our gurus, brothers and sisters are our gurus, lovers are our gurus, friends are our gurus and even our enemies are our gurus. Even *things* can be our gurus. Like the internet, for example, when it's crawling along slower than a slug, that's when I think I should maybe have more patience. I mean, really when you look at it, isn't everything teaching us something? In fact, the whole of existence is our guru; it's like one almighty Zen stick which just keeps whacking us over the head until we wake up and smell the coffee.

Anyway, this book is not about finding a guru or me being your guru, it's about learning from the guru of life itself. Indeed, existence may be the purest guru of all, as it leaves you to your own devices and doesn't tell you what to do, then conveniently highlights the consequences of your actions and gently points the way through. No, I am not a god or a guru, I'm just little ol' me, sharing with little ol' u, pointing to the big ol' U beyond. And if you really must pin a label on me, then consider me a friend who is only too aware of the trials and tribulations of life.

G.U.R.U is a book about YOU. I know at times it may seem to be about me, but I'm only using me to illustrate you, and ultimately of course, there's no me and there's no you. See, my thinking is, if I can show you who I am, then maybe I can show you who you are. Then once you get clear about you and start seeing the cosmic joke, then we can have a good old laugh together!

Chapter 1

I Celebrate Myself: God Is No Where, Life Is Now Here

"Enlightenment is not something to be achieved; it is just to be lived. When I say that I achieved enlightenment, I simply mean that I decided to live it. Enough is enough! And since then I have lived it. It is a decision that now you are not interested in creating problems – that's all. It is a decision that now you are finished with all this nonsense of creating problems and finding solutions. All this nonsense is a game you are playing with yourself: you yourself are hiding and you yourself are seeking, you are both the parties. And you know it! You understand it. It has to be so because it is your own game: you are hiding and waiting for yourself to be able to seek and find yourself."

Ancient Music in the Pines, Osho

By now, you're probably wondering, who is this Krishna Prem guy, and why is he qualified to tell me about me? So, let me introduce you to "Gee, I am me!" Right from day one on planet earth, I was a seeker and a rebel. I felt I was searching for something and I felt I was different, different not only from all the other kids I knew, but different also from even my own brothers and sisters. I don't know, maybe everyone feels that way? But I definitely felt odd, like some kind of misfit. Maybe it was because I was the youngest of six children and my parents were much older than my friends' parents, although I had a pretty normal kind of name – Michael.

I remember hearing that my elder sister wanted to get married but my mother, who was pregnant with me at the time,

1

embarrassingly said to her, "Could you at least wait until Michael is born?" So I was born into a family with a sister who was nineteen years older than me and a mother who was nineteen years older than her. Immediately after I was born, my elder sister got married and went off to live her own life, while my mother found out she had breast cancer and became aware that she was going to die.

There I was, a one year-old baby when my mother died, and my second elder sister, Phyllis, took all the responsibility of raising me. Of course I don't have any conscious memories of my birth mother, but I do have many memories of my sister, whom I called Mum, and my wonderful loving relationship with her. But from my belly, even as a baby, even though I loved her like a mother, I knew she wasn't my real mother. My father, who was a wealthy man in a small town, basically a big fish in a small pond, insisted that my sister-mother stayed home and didn't go out to work, so she could cultivate a good relationship with me. So you can see how quirky the situation was; my father was my father, my mother was my sister, but my mother was also the daughter of my father! And of course, because my "parents" weren't husband and wife, they didn't behave like husband and wife, so when the going got rough, which happened a lot, they never kissed and made up or let off steam through makeup sex.

So, even though I had a comfortable childhood, I didn't have a normal upbringing; and even though I felt a certain love and caring from my sister-mother, I didn't feel that unconditional love and acceptance that only a mother knows how to give. Then when I was aged nine, my father died, and I remember feeling a tremendous sense of relief that he wasn't going to be around anymore, and that now I could be alone with my sister-mother. My father and I had never really been close, and I think it was basically

2

"Accept yourself as you are." Osho

because he was trying so hard to not get in the way. But I do recall he would often look me in the eye and say, "Someday, I'm going to teach you everything I know!" That day never came.

It was only years and years later, that I thought, "My god! Perhaps, I should not have been so happy about not having parents!" Maybe other kids might have felt really upset about not having their parents around, but for me it felt somehow OK. Perhaps that's why I always thought of myself as a little strange, as a bit of a madman, because somehow I always seemed to do everything backwards in life, always seemed to look at things upside-down. I was always laughing when others were crying or seeing the humor in something quite dark. And I think that's why I started questioning life so early and why I went on this search.

As I say, right from early childhood, I was curious about life. I was always asking questions about where I came from and where everyone else came from too, for that matter. I recall when I was thirteen years old, the local rabbi kept telling me that God was Jewish, that he, the rabbi, was Jewish and that I, Michael, was Jewish too! And instead of just saying yes and keeping quiet, I kept on asking him, "But who was God before he became Jewish? But who were you before you became a rabbi?" And bypassing my questions completely, he used to answer, "That's none of your business. Just get a good education, become a lawyer and marry a nice Jewish girl." And even though I didn't like his line at all, just by trotting off to business school I was already biting the bullet.

Off I went and got a good education, did the BSc thing and duly graduated from business school. I did the whole fandango, but my god, it wasn't me. I mean, I just wasn't interested in how the world began or the signing of the Magna Carta in the year 1512 or was it 1215? I wasn't interested in what happened hundreds or thousands

3

or millions of years ago. I didn't care about sixteenth-century period dress or what the dinosaurs ate for lunch. I was only interested in where I came from and who I was. Deep down, I thought that everyone else was too. Don't get me wrong, I don't think education is a bad thing, I think it's only natural to want to learn about all the weird and wonderful things in this world, and it's only natural to want to learn about ourselves too!

I had an education problem and I had a weight problem. I had a prescription for diet pills and I would pop those diet pills and grind my teeth and take long walks and just think about life. I was interested in how I got here and who I am. I guess we all are; the longing to know who we are at the same time as we are moving forward with our education. It's quite a thing being a young man.

Many times when I would come back from India and visit my family and suggest something I learned in the East that I had never heard in the West, I had some really fun experiences. For example I was saying to my sister Margie that in the East in the Sufi tradition we say that if a man dies with five friends, when you hold up your hand each finger represents a friend and you hold up your hand and the Sufi master says to you, "If you leave your body having had five friends you had a successful life." And my sister Margie looked at me and said, "Your mother always said that to you." And it's cute because I never heard my sister-mother say it to me, so she must have mentioned that to me when I was a teenager in heat because obviously if she had said it to me in my first twelve years, there is a very good chance I would remember that. You know I can remember that I never learnt anything as a child. Nobody told me anything except be a child. I just did not have any sense of being; only being young. I never had a chance to think that I was already who I am.

4

So, my way of dealing with my education problem and my weight problem was to just pop a few pills, go for these long walks and contemplate life. But the questioning didn't go away. The search didn't stop; it just went on and on, for years and years!

I remember when I was twenty-eight years old I left for London to be a legal drug-dealer; I became a bartender for two years before going to India. I didn't say a word to my family about going further. Even going to Europe was a big risk in their eyes. So while I was in India, I would write postcards as if I was in London or Paris. I would then find someone who was actually going to those places, to send them home to my family, just so they wouldn't get worried or nervous.

I never heard anyone say, "I feel therefore I am," but if they did, I would also have to say, that's bullshit! And I say that from experience. For most of my life I thought my feelings were me! I thought I was moodiness incarnate, a happy-sad clown with more than my fair share of ups and downs. And at one particular time in my life I thought I was my self-loathing and self-hate. It was a miserable time, which I refer to as "my war with me," and it began when I was called up by the U.S. Army to go and fight in Vietnam.

The thing was I didn't want to fight. I couldn't find one good reason to fight, or any enemy worth fighting. In fact, the only fight I was willing to fight, was against my own army! So I went through that whole process they call a court-martial and it was all very difficult because I was in the U.S. Army Reserves at the time, well, at least until I was deemed insane by an army psychiatrist, and promptly thrown out. Now the Catch 22 situation here is that when you're thrown out of the U.S. Army Reserves, you're automatically thrown into the U.S. Army. Only the U.S. Army didn't want me either because I was, after all, insane.

5

I went through five years of confusion while the powers that be decided what to do with me. As you can imagine, this was not a happy period of my life, and my thoughts and feelings were all over the place. I mean, I didn't want to fight anyone, but on the other hand, I wasn't thrilled about not fighting for my country either. And... I didn't want to meet the enemy, but on the other hand, maybe this enemy had something to teach me. So there I was; I didn't want the army, the army didn't want me, but I also didn't want a black mark on my record. In the end, it took five years for the army to grant me an honorable discharge, and to this day I am proud of how my papers read: "Michael Mogul is unable to adjust to the military lifestyle." You got that right guys!

So I took my papers and flew to London, England, where the only job I could get was as a bartender. There I poured drink after drink for the customers, and drink after drink for me, until before long I was happily unconscious along with everyone else in the bar. Many of my customers were really beautiful people, guys I had a lot of respect for, guys that had fought in World War II and had had half their faces blown off. You could still see the burn marks all over their bodies. And as I began to relate with them, I began to feel more and more jealous that they had been willing to fight for their country, that they had felt blessed by their country and that they were able to drink and enjoy their country, while I, on the other hand, had been unable to do what my country had asked of me. As I talked with these guys my misery and pain went deeper and deeper until one day I couldn't handle it anymore. So I got really, really drunk, bought a one-way ticket, and got on the available first plane to India. Well, it wasn't quite as accidental as that, because you see, when you work till two in the morning in England, generally the only places still open to go and get a bite to eat at that time are Indian restaurants. I ended up going for copious

6

amounts of Indian meals and loving the food and loving the people, until one day, as I say, instead of going to the restaurant I just hopped on a plane!

The bar-tending job was at The Ship Hotel in Shepperton, a bedroom of London. I was only now working nights which gave me an opportunity to make some money during the day. So I took a job as a hod-carrier which meant that I was carrying six bricks at a time up, and sometimes down, a ladder. In a matter of weeks I became muscle-bound. I was five foot nine tall when I started the job, and I was five foot nine wide when I boarded the plane for India. I looked like a brick shithouse.

My first job with Osho was as one of his bodyguards. I didn't protect his body so much, but I always seemed to be carrying his chair up and down the podium where he spoke. The further East you get, the taller five foot nine is, and certainly muscles didn't exist in India because it requires a lot of hard work.

At this point Osho was calling together his disciples for meditation camps, which were held all around India, so I decided to visit Nepal for one month, in between two of these camps. The Himalayas are considered young mountains and, in fact, are still growing. Having met my first god-man in India I was overwhelmed by the absolute beauty of these baby peaks. For me being in the Himalayas was like seeing god, god's work in action. Having been a city boy all my life my definition of clean was an un-opened Coca-Cola® can in the supermarket; I'd never seen nature au naturel before. I'm the kind of guy that went to the Himalayas before I visited the Rocky Mountains back home in America, again reminding you that my life lessons began by being as far away from my upbringing as possible. By now I know if I can know one rose totally, all the secrets of the universe will be

be a criminal." Osho

revealed, but as a young man in heat I needed to freeze my ass off on the top of the world. For one month I lived on rice and beans and chai (Indian tea) and I was so delighted with life that I didn't know I had become delirious with dysentery. I completely lost all of the muscle that I had gained as a hod-carrier. The only thing that remained was the pot-belly I was born with and will die with, my little buddha-belly has been a constant in my life. When I returned to see Osho, I've never seen his eyes so big as when he saw how small my body had become. I felt I looked very cute without that extra thirty pounds slowing me down. I wasn't given the chair-carrying job again.

One thing is that it wasn't just the mountains that were so beautiful; it was also the Nepalese people; the biggest thing about them is their smile, and as one Nepalese man told me, "It takes less muscles to smile than to frown."

When it became time to return to Osho, I ran down the mountain all the way for twenty kilometers, sliding on the soft pebbles almost like I was skiing.

At the Ship Hotel we had a small bar upstairs for after-hours drinking. The hotel had six bedrooms and four bars and the six bedrooms were for the clients of the four bars. It reached a point where the customers went beyond their conditioning and no longer knew they were English. For twenty-five quid plus tax they could figure out who they were tomorrow morning. The difference between meditation and inebriation is awareness, but before I actually understood this, even as a bartender I had a judgment about alcohol. When a customer got really plastered I would oftentimes guess how long it would take for him to scrape the plaster off the wall and have to be helped to bed. The difference, now that I'm a great meditator, is that I have become aware that

8

"Look not for the body, but somebody's being. Watch, explore. Sooner or later

intoxication is a birthright, that sometimes it's just great to leave the world behind you. For me, again, the difference between one too many and being aware of oneness is meditation. If I hadn't met Osho, I fully believe I would have become my own best customer. I'll drink to that.

Getting back to the point, one night before I put a customer to bed, he changed the words from the song "He's got the whole world in his hands" to "I have the whole world in my hand." It's not a big story, but I can only say I remember judging this man even though I was an atheist at the time, as being absolutely arrogant. Welcome back to Western conditioning. So you can imagine when I got to the East how shocked I was to read what Ramana Maharshi is quoted as saying, "You don't appear in the world, the world appears in you." When you are shocked in the East by a god-man, you also judge as if he is a drunkard, but you learn to trust that there is a grain of truth in this drunk.

Could it possibly be true that the world appears in you instead of you appearing in the world? I ask you this 'cause I am meditating on this still, so I can't give you any answer. But I can ask you this question, "Did you exist before your conditioning, or did you appear with your conditioning intact?" In other words who were you from age nine months before you were born to three years after you were born? Before you learnt to say "no" your parents filled you up with their fear and their untruth and their religion until there was no room for you. So ever since you were three years old, all you have ever done is agree with the stuff that filled you up in every nook and cranny of your body, mind and spirit, or you rebelled against all of this without trusting who you are. The words meditation and medication come from the same root. You take medication to get healthy; you take meditation to get back to who you were before your parents make love. I know

9

you will find somebody who fits with you." Osho

it'll piss you off, but you haven't had an honest moment, a naked moment, since the moment before your parents made love. You are the best robot ever created by your parents and your priests and your politicians. And if that doesn't make you feel like shit, meet me at the Ship Hotel and don't wait for me, just start drinking.

I stood on my sister-mother's doorstep, wearing orange pajamas and a string of wooden beads round my neck (which was what all disciples of Osho were wearing at that time), a beard to my knees, wild, crazy hair and my eyes aglow, looking thousands of years old – basically unrecognizable to the real world. Shitting my pants, I rang the doorbell. When my mother opened the door, she first looked me up and down and then she said, "I always knew this was going to happen to you!"

This is, I imagine, what all parents say when they have a strong feeling about how their kids are going to turn out. And there I was, thinking it was going to be such a shock for her, but it wasn't, it wasn't shocking at all. You know, it's pretty hard to fool your mother. Besides, she'd always known that I wasn't interested in material things and that the only thing I'd ever been curious about was who I was and where I'd come from. In a strange way, I loved what she said to me, because it meant she really knew me. My sister-mother explained to me that it was always difficult for her because I would never ask simple things like how much is two plus two, I would always ask where did I come from and where was I going? And even when I became a man in the Jewish religion at thirteen, I was never satisfied with the robot answers of my teaching rabbi. In fact she herself said to me that she had a past life in Egypt. I remember laughing when she said that and asking her the same question Osho asked me, which is when are you gonna give up the past and the future for the present. Basically when Osho asked me this question my inner voice said my answer would

10

bore the shit out of you. Isn't it funny how exciting everything is except being in the present? At least, that's the way it was for me before I met Osho.

I can imagine how surprised my sister-mother was when her only son Brian was just as bananas as me. He was born with one of his lower vertebrae missing. At age twenty-one, while he was still a senior in college, he was scheduled to have an operation on his back, followed by a full-body cast for one year. A friend of his who was a college professor came to visit Brian just hours before the operation and offered to help him relax through hypnosis. Brian was amazed how deeply relaxed he felt at the end of one hour of deep hypnosis. He got off the operating table, looked at his professor and said, "I'm going to pursue this avenue of healing." He took his college degree in psychology, got on a motorcycle and drove across country to meet Dr. Milton Erickson, the father of modern hypnosis.

Milton Erickson had suffered from polio for years in the same area of his back that Brian was suffering. Erickson said to my brother that he would take him as his last student if Brian agreed to get a PhD in psychology and join a gym. Erickson said that without a doctorate of psychology no one would take Brian seriously and without going to a gym and building up his stomach muscles his back would not give him a chance to heal. Brian went on to become a giant in the field of self-hypnosis and also went from a ninety-pound weakling to a Charles Atlas look-alike. Brian and Milton would often do pain-control work through hypnosis simultaneously, and thus Erickson became a friend as well as a mentor. One thing I remember distinctly is that Milton Erickson said to my brother Brian, "We can reduce your pain from one hundred percent to ten percent and that ten percent would become your guru. If your pain goes up to twenty-five percent, stop helping

11

freedom, and lust simply creates prisons for you." Osho

other people through hypnosis and remember to work on yourself."
This measure still holds true after thirty-five years.

You can imagine my sister-mother when I stayed with Osho
and went deep into meditation and my brother gave himself to a
crackpot named Dr. Milton Erickson; one of her sons went East
and one of her sons went West. I bet she wished she was back in
Egypt when the two of us came to dinner at the same time. By now
Brian had his PhD in psychology and I had birthed Geetam for
Osho. Brian was living in San Diego and would drive his
motorcycle up my driveway to have dinner with me on his way to
see Erickson, taking off just after midnight that same evening and
riding through the night on his way to Arizona where Erickson
lived. I remember he would join Erickson for breakfast and Brian
always felt that Dr. Erickson wouldn't make it through the day he
looked so bad. Erickson would excuse himself after breakfast to do
an hour of self-hypnosis so he could get through the day, and he
suggested that Brian do the same. It was amazing to Brian that
Erickson would come out at nine o'clock and see clients for eight
hours while Brian observed the work. Erickson would be totally
alive and giving for eight hours. At the end of the day Erickson
would again collapse into near death and that's just the way he
worked. I remember Brian once saying to me that Milton asked
him, "What did you think of the manic depressive we worked with
today?" And Brian scratched his head because he didn't know the
answer and Milton said it was the first couple that he had seen that
morning: the husband was manic and the wife was depressive.
Brian remained a student of Erickson's until Erickson passed
away.

Years later I was with Osho in Pune when I found out that my
sister-mother was dying from ALS, also known as Lou Gehrig's
disease. I went for a leaving darshan with Osho quite suddenly as I

"They say that God is everywhere, and yet we always think of Him as somewhat

wanted to go home and pay my respects. I mentioned to Osho that my mother and I often chanted together, and I asked him if it would be appropriate to chant the sound of silence, AUM, with her – I wanted to have a simple chant as she was having trouble breathing. Osho said it would be much better to chant O because he said in such a sensitive period as imminent death it's better not to fake life, and to simply chant of the letter O would bring amazing results, and would be more honest. So here I am now, sitting in my mother's hospital room, chanting the sound of O. She was unable to join me, but there was no question we could feel each other. It was all a bit overwhelming for me, and when the nurse came by to bathe her, I found myself alone in the adjacent bathroom. Sitting on the toilet I continued to chant O and the pain and the frustration and the love that I was feeling transformed the sound of O into the song of AUM. I composed myself, went back to my mother and just held her hand in silence. In America dying takes forever. We keep each other alive through medicine, more through medicine than through meditation. I was needed back at Geetam and my older brother Max drove me to the airport to pick up the Red Eye to LA for about ninety-nine dollars one-way. My brother suggested that even though we had insurance for my mother, everyone in the family was being asked to chip in one hundred dollars a month. I knew in my heart of hearts that there was only going to be one month, so I reached into my pocket when we got to the airport, and I gave my brother my last one-hundred-dollar bill. He asked if I wanted him to stay until my airplane was ready and I said if it was OK with him I'd rather be alone. As his car drove off I put out my thumb and I hitch-hiked from Orlando International Airport, the home of Disney World, and headed west for Disneyland. And even though my real name was Michael Mogul, in moments like this I actually felt more like Mickey Mouse – death is so surreal. My mother's death just felt unreal.

of a recluse." Emily Dickenson

Since I didn't have any money to sleep, I hitch-hiked just over three thousand miles in just over three days. My mother left her body before I had to raise another hundred dollars.

As you can see, I was always more focused on the big picture, on existence itself, rather than the little, local me. Somehow, I had always known that there was more to life than met the eye. Somehow, unlike my father who had been happy with his little pond, I had always felt there was a much bigger pond to swim in. And I share this with you, not because you need to do what I did, suddenly drop everything and go to India to find a guru, although if the truth be told, you don't find them, they find you. That's what I did, that's what I needed, but maybe you need something different? Maybe what you need is to crawl around on the ground like a small child and just explore everything as if it's brand new. Or maybe what you need is five years of full-on therapy, or to visit the oldest, longest beard in the Himalayas and ask him to share the mysteries of the universe with you? I don't know. Only you know what you need; only you know what works for you.

Like I say, I'm not encouraging you to be a weirdo or a drop-out, just to step back a little from your everyday world and question life itself and who you really are. You don't have to do thirty years in India to do that; you can do it just sitting in your armchair. You don't have to have a guru to do that, just an open mind and a sense of humor. We're all heading out and we're all heading home, and although we're all travelling on different trains, we're all going to end up in the same railway station.

Well, I have had many places in this world and you always have to turn on the gas. So in Boston when the gasman comes over to turn on the gas and you get to bullshitting with him over a cup of coffee and you say, "Hey, is this your life?" and he says, "No, as a

"We can live without religion and meditation, but we cannot survive without

matter of fact at night I am going to Boston University to get my masters in art history. I would like to become a professor one day." Everyone in Boston, no matter what they are doing, is thinking about becoming a PhD. Now you go to California, to Los Angeles, and you get yourself a little place and you get the gasman in, you make him a cup of herb tea and you say, "Hey, what is going on? Is this who you are?" and he says, "Absolutely not, at night I am writing a movie script. I wanna be a writer in Hollywood and someday I wanna be a director. The best way to become a director is coming through being a writer." Aha, so you know everybody in LA is going to be an actor, is going to be a writer and if they are not everybody wants them to consider that because they have the talent at least to be a character actor.

I spent many years in Europe working and having girlfriends and in Europe when you say to somebody you are a friend of mine, they really look at you funny because to be a friend of somebody in Europe takes a long time. They have different words for different kinds of friends and they were always shocked when I immediately referred to them as friends within days of having a cup of coffee or within moments of having a good fuck. The girl would look to me and say, "You know, you are moving too fast. It's OK that we made love but it's certainly not OK that we're friends." It's just different there. And I love it when Europeans go to America and they are walking on a crossing, lots of traffic, the light is about to turn red, they are just about to get hit by a speeding car and an absolute stranger looks at them and says, "How are you today?" My god, Europeans almost get killed when they hear that question for the first time because they are ready to speak, they are ready to give an answer. How am I? This is how I am. They have absolutely no idea that this does not mean that at all. When you ask the question as an American, you simply aren't

15

human affection." Dalai Lama

waiting for an answer, it's just another greeting. Why say a word back? And until Europeans get used to that question they are absolutely in a gap.

And years later when I did finally return to Boston, I returned in orange pajamas which all sannyasins at the time were wearing, and I had a beard that reached my pubic hair and I looked just absolutely wild and my eyes were aglow and I was in love, but I was broke of course and I had to go back to the States and maybe make some money and stay alive. And shitting my pants, I rang the front door bell and my mother came to the door and she looked at me and she said "I always knew this was going to happen to you." It's pretty hard to fool the mother. I know that people that come to the East think it's a very creative gesture and when they look for a master and the master says. "You know, it's really not up to you, I was actually calling you and you are responding to my call." I loved it because somewhere the mother also always knows, "My god, I have a strange boy in my house. He is not asking about anything except who he is, where did he come from, where is he going; does not seem at all interested in the material world. What came through me?" So that's what I really loved when she said, "I always knew this was going to happen to you," because somewhere she was one of the few people in my life that knew what was going to happen to me. It was not shocking at all, not shocking at all.

And I remember a very strange story. I had two sisters that did not talk to each other and I was about sixteen at the time. I had a driver's license and of course I did not own a car and sometimes both of my sisters would lend me their car because they were naughty girls and they remembered when they were sixteen how much fun it is to take a joy ride. But the only time neither one of them would lend me their car is when I wanted to visit the other

16

sister. They just weren't in love with each other at the time. So what happened for me is I used to have to hitchhike if I was at one sister's house and I wanted to see the other sister's house. And my most favorite time was when a girl named Elinor picked me up when I was hitchhiking and she turned out to be my first girlfriend. Now I am fifty years old and I am going to visit the two sisters and even though now they were getting along actually, they just did not have time to lend me the car.

So there I was, a fifty-year-old guy with a long beard and graying hair and now I am in maroon pajamas and I am just hitch-hiking and I wanna say hello. I am not in a rush. It doesn't really make a difference and all of a sudden a thought comes into my mind. I hope Elinor picks me up. Wouldn't that be funny? Now I haven't seen her in thirty years, I don't know where she lives, I don't know what she looks like. I know that she got married at least once because she married the next boy after me and actually she left me for him. I will never forgive her even though I am fifty now, that's a terrible thing to do Elinor. Anyway, my god, all of a sudden a station wagon with a good-looking woman and two children in the back seat, makes a U-turn and picks me up and it's Elinor. We both went into shock, we both went into laughter, we both remembered how we felt the first time we met. There was still energy in the car; of course we did not need to move on it. But it was really cute. There was still that thing that two young people have when they first meet each other. Anyway, it was freaky. By the way, I am not making any claims about being psychic by having meditation, and you don't get psychic abilities just because you meditate.

No, I am not saying that at all. It was just a coincidence and one of those moments when you just remember and you feel like sharing in a book if you ever write one. Believe it or not, she picks

17

me up and she took me right to my sister, she knew exactly where I was going. It was hilarious and we had such a good laugh and of course she just got divorced and she has just started to date somebody new and I don't know what happened, we never stayed in touch after that. It was a moment, I am sure you have all had one of those.

My mother died early, my father died early. Even Phyllis died early. I will never forget it, I turned fifty years old and I was still alive and I went, "Oh my god, I am going to have to look at my life." I can remember when I met Osho, that feeling that the path of meditation is good for me because there is no way that I am going to ever outgrow being dysfunctional in a family situation. But there I am fifty; I am still alive and there I am. I had to do what we call primal: I had to look at my life from the basement up. So there is nobody in the room with me when I am doing my primal therapy that is still alive. My father is not here, my mother is not here, my sister-mother is not here; even my guru had left his body by then. I had so much to work on and not only that, but anybody that has done primal knows how terrible it is and after a few days of primal the therapist said, "We are going to have to start all over again because your life is so mixed up and I am finally understanding how much we need to separate your two mothers so that you can see your relationship with both these women independently."

I will always remember that we were playing kids games one day, just being kids. The therapist said, "You know, you have never been a kid. Basically one of the situations in your life, especially with no parents, is that you have a memory of needing to take care of yourself even as a baby. So we will need to play and see what we can come up with when we play, maybe we can get in touch with your feeling." We were just playing with several balls of yarn. There was a big circle and my real mother was at one end

18

of the circle, just a ball of yarn on the ground, and I was just a ball of yarn on the ground. We were just two little balls of yarn in this lifetime in one big circle. We could see a big piece of yarn that was my sister-mother separating those two balls of yarn; in fact it went from one end of the universe to the other. And that was my sister-mother and I just picked up that piece of yarn and I kind of made a little ball out of it and I threw the ball out of the circle. Now there were just these two balls of yarn and for the very first time in my life I felt my mother. Now I had no memories of her like you and I might have when we meet. In other words I did not remember anything, but all of a sudden this physical sensation came over me where I could relate with my real mother for the very first time, I could feel her for the very first time. Would you call it esoteric? Would you call it unbelievable that a son could feel his mother for the very first time even though he was fifty years old? And I know maybe you might even feel sad for me, but there was an absolute sense of joy to finally feel her. I would say that absolute sense of joy was also mixed up with sadness but I was already past that, I never expected to experience her at all and there was a certain delight in feeling her and loving her and playing with her and experiencing her pain that she was leaving her family. Obviously I was feeling her love for my father and the wanting to relate with him as she was dying, more than she wanted to relate with me. These are all interpretations of course but the feeling was there of finally feeling oneness. You might say, "Oh poor little Krishna Prem, poor little Mikey, what a difficult time this must have been for him, this moment." But it wasn't, because I actually feel that she needed to say goodbye to more people than just to me. She had been with my father now for twenty-five years, she had had six children with him, and she was leaving. She was leaving and also she had given me over to my sister. This was my feeling and you know I could be completely wrong again, even about feeling, never

Have you heard about the dyslexic yogi who goes around chanting "MO?"

mind about spirituality, but here I am, she gave me over to my sister, she did not want to get in the way of that relationship happening. I think what she might not have known is that I could never have the feeling that my sister-mother was actually my mother. I could hide behind that as kind of dessert. I always call that love dessert because I think it takes a real mother to give you a main course.

Now you could go ahead and close this book saying, "My god I am reading a book about meditation from a man that never had a mother." But you know what; you never had a mother either. You think you had a mother and you are attached to it that this woman is a mother but again I wanna remind you that there is no you to have a mother. There is no mother to have a son or a daughter. There is gratitude, there are bodies, there is life, but there is no you. I know you are not gonna believe this and you are gonna have to spend some time meditating even to find out if what I am saying is true or full of shit. But what I am saying is that you exist as a witness only, that you exist as god only. But you are seeing and feeling this through your body.

So it's very, very simply to get identified with this body and call it "it" and protect it and take care of it and be pissed off with when life isn't treating you good, to be happy when life is treating you good. I don't know what to say. I would rather be rich and healthy than poor and sick but you can go on and on and see that I am telling the truth right now, that you need to remember the witness. That you need to see that you were here the whole time and that right now you're here-ness is about being a man, about being a woman, about being American or wherever you're from. These are just labels that you have wanted to believe in so much that they become you. That you cannot see that you are a tree yet you feel like you are a forest. You have to get back to who you really are.

20

"Be, don't try to become. Within these two words, be and becoming,

So when I did this primal you might say, "Oh my god, he is on the ground crying," but basically I was on the ground celebrating. I loved reconnecting with my mother. I loved saying, "Thank you for bringing me here." I loved saying that everything that was not good in my life brought me to everything that is good in my life.

And that is being in love with the master and meditation and again you hear the cosmic joke. She just laughed back at me, "You are such an idiot, in essence it's all a joke. You need to wake up." There is no guarantee that Krishna Prem in love with the master is going to awaken any more than a housewife in New Jersey with three children just getting through the day. It can happen to anyone, anytime, anywhere.

Let's just say my job was simply to go to India and let's just say that I just walked into a bank and I have met the president of the bank and I ask him a question about money and he says, "Well, I have thirty years of experience and I can help you to invest in the right way." Well of course he is not gonna tell you that, he has had some ups and downs and sometimes he is right and sometimes he is wrong. He is just gonna call it experience. I have had some ups and downs but this is what I learned: how to handle those ups and downs. That I am not up and I am not down. I am seeing, I am witnessing upping and downing. And I want to point out as best as I can that there is no such thing as waves, there is only the ocean waving. There is no such thing as Krishna Prem, there is only existence appearing right now as Krishna Prem. Pretty heady stuff, pretty heartfelt stuff, pretty belly stuff. Basically we need to trust ourselves. We need to be here and now.

Having no mother changes many things in your conditioning. For example, I was raised by one sister and my father, and as a child I would watch them fight and then go to separate rooms. In

your whole life is contained." Osho

my world, fights didn't resolve with sex. Now some of my friends say that the best sex is after a fight. I don't know. It doesn't happen like that for me.

Everybody has their own formula about sex. Sex is sex is sex. Here's where I feel really blessed. In this life, sex has been my payoff... to the point where I have no fantasies left. And that's really a major thing for a man. So, in fact, I'm overpaid.

I fell in love with a master who is in love with women. There is simply no way I would have had so many lovers without Osho. I knew it was a blessing. All these beautiful women who came to him, it wasn't like I attracted them. He attracted them. In my whole life I never looked in the mirror and said, "She needs me." When I met Osho, I met five thousand buddhas who looked like sisters to me.

One deceptive thing about me is that I look like a man, but I'm not so sure. Having been born into a family with so much female energy, sometimes I act like a woman. For example, when the going gets tough, I go shopping! But a long time ago I decided I was not willing to make the same "mistake" as my father, who had a knack for creating a rival sibling every three times he made love. So, I got my tubes tied and went to bed with all of my sannyas sisters.

And through this abundance of women in my life, thanks to Osho, and through my acceptance of women as friends, I've reached the psychological highlight where it's okay if I'm a bad fuck. I wish I could say that sex has dropped me. In fact, it hasn't. And to balance this statement, I also have to say that sex is not my boss anymore either.

"Anyone who says he can see through women is missing a lot." Groucho Marx

We've all heard that a man thinks about sex every three minutes, and a woman every six. Well, Krishna is up to four minutes now! As a young man I used to be hard before my female friend knocked on the door. Now I get hard after she leaves. In between these two experiences is a moment of balance. In those moments, I celebrate with a cup of tea and a cuddle.

I guess every man since midlife asks himself, "Do I miss the drive?" The answer is yes. My sexual drive is no longer a primal scream. Now sex is as much a thank you as a tension reliever.

It has taken my whole life to understand the fear around relationship – that women want a main course from a man. They want to be taken seriously. They want steak and potatoes, and all I could ever be was a friend; I could only offer tiramisu. Now I understand.

I'm in a relationship right now. Her name is Jwala, which means fire. This relationship is burning me up. It scares me. My beloved was brought up by four brothers and no father. And that's where we regress, directly into two kids that need each other. The difference I see between sex and relationship is that relationship puts me in the unknown. Right now love helps me to live there – otherwise I'd run.

And here is a little story to keep you cool, that I wrote for Viha Connection Magazine. It's called "Looking for Miss Take," by Krishna Prem, also known as Mister Right.

I was not brought up to be alone. My purpose here on planet Earth, according to my family (meaning Mum), was to meet my soul mate (as long as she was Jewish), get married, and have babies in order to carry on the family name – and then naturally

"I am having a bad 'here' day." Yogini

health, wealth, and happiness would follow. I could go on for lifetimes explaining how this scenario has a tragic ending, but I imagine you can fill in the blanks out of your own experience. No matter whether you are Mr. Right or Miss Take, love is chock full of tragic endings.

Allow me to go deep for a moment. Love that seeks another is destined to fail. Love that finds his or her own self is destined to be love in the here and now, not in the future. In the words of Buddha, enjoyed by Osho, and stolen by me: Love yourself and watch.

When I met Osho, it was a wake-up call. He reminded me in no uncertain words to drop loneliness and to live in my aloneness. My inner voice sang out, "Goodness gracious, great balls of fire!" I walked out of this particular darshan with Osho in '75 complete unto myself. As I staggered out of his room, I bumped into his garden full of delicious women. I got confused all over again. My god, in those days there were three women for every man. Aloneness quickly took a backseat. I was able to give up my mother's concept of marriage, but my manliness was excited to the max, and my loneliness was so covered up with lust that I simply had no idea that I was not getting Osho's point.

Through the following years of trial and error I have come to the understanding that aloneness is who I am and loneliness is simply aloneness without a center. So allow me one moment here to say, "I am
sorry" to those ladies whom I loved and lost along the way from here to here. This is it.

Let me make it perfectly clear; ladies, hold up your index fingers. And gentlemen, hold up high your middle fingers. Now

"Life is short. Kiss slowly, laugh insanely, love truly and forgive quickly."

ladies, is there anything you would like to say to all the middle fingers on this planet? For example, "Go fuck yourself!" I, for one middle finger, can handle anything you want to say because after all is said and done, we are all fingers of one hand. And as fingers of one hand, there is no such thing as separation. We are one hand appearing as two fingers.

How does a guy like me hit the wall? After I had dated for years and years in the ashram, the commune, and finally in the Meditation Resort, and had never met Miss Right, it finally dawned on me that I must be Mister Wrong. So instead of running out to the Cappuccino Bar to make a date I found myself dancing alone at Kundalini Meditation. I could have continued blaming all the Miss Takes in the world but until I cleaned up my own act, love was just an impossible dream.

The real Miss Take was meeting my friend Jwala. We fell in love, and I absolutely did not change. This was not good enough for her. She insisted that if we actually wanted to give our love a chance, I could either have a frontal lobotomy or enroll in Primal Therapy followed by Co-Dependency and Path of Love. Or she would leave me. I broke up with her immediately.   A month later, I came to my senses, begged her to come back to me, and against my better judgment agreed to embark on a crash course of therapy. In therapy I was confronted with this character KP, with his wild mood swings, and I had to look at his life and love affairs. Then I got that these cyclones are on the periphery and the real me is at the center.

What a Miss Take Jwala turned out to be! We have been together for fifteen years now. We're still not married, still making love without having

Paulo Coelho

children, and still growing together. We're simply being together. For me, this feeling of oneness with a beloved allowed me for the first time to experience my aloneness, not my loneliness.

For me, Osho pointed out the truth – but who gives a shit until the truth is "Who I am?" So scream away, love away, lonely away… whatever it takes to love out of your aloneness. For now, I don't know what it feels like to be a center without a cyclone, but I can say from my very center that Miss Take never felt so good. So allow me one more moment to say to Miss Take, as well as Mr. Right, that I love you until the "I" and the "you" disappear, and only love remains.

It's easier for me now to be super-conscious than sexy. In fact, as I am watching myself say all this, I can hear myself telling all the women I've been with: Thank you. And to all the women who said no: I'm coming back as a blonde Gina Lollobrigida (Osho's favorite) in my next life – I won't be as available! As one of Osho's friends who still lives in Pune, in the Resort itself, I find it difficult to use the word super-conscious without thinking I am competing with the master. But if super-consciousness means being aware that you've been touched by the master and his female disciples, then this does describe me, and I feel grateful.

And I also feel quite mature, even though this expression grows out of a history of being premature all my life. But who I am now is not interested in being premature or mature. Now in my life I'm always watching the point where I tip, looking for the place where I am neither one. This is what I call aloneness. Ironically, sex is not my door to enlightenment, but my door to aloneness. It is no longer a biological thing, but a way of getting into my aloneness. Sex has helped me to be alone.

"Being is enlightenment, becoming is ignorance." Osho

When I speak about sex to friends now, the conversation has just as much to do with the peaks and valleys of relating as to wrestling with the eternal esoteric question of tits and ass. The beloved helps me to fall in love with myself as well. And I am still thrilled to say that I didn't learn all my lessons about being a man on the football field – I'd rather touch you than touchdown!

In the introduction to the reprint of Osho's book,The Goose Is Out, I wrote about my evolving understanding of this famous Zen metaphor.

When I was a young man and had never been kissed, I was in love with America's favorite pastime – baseball. The score was tied eight-eight when the game was called because of darkness, and I suddenly realized I was in deep trouble on the home front.

By the time I made it home, dinner was well over. My older sister Margie met me at the front screen door and said, "Mum wants to see you in her room right away." As I struggled to get past her she whispered in my ear, "Your goose is cooked."

And even though my virgin ears had never heard this expression before, I knew exactly what she meant. Older sisters are wicked Zen Masters. Years later, long after my dream of playing baseball for the Boston Red Sox had gone up in smoke, I fell in love with another Zen Master, Osho, who gave me the same message with a slightly different twist: "Your goose is out!"

You see, there is a beautiful Zen story about a goose that's put in a bottle when it is very young. It grows up in the bottle and eventually gets too big to take out. The koan which has been driving Zen monks crazy for the past several hundred years is: How do you get the goose out of the bottle without either killing the goose or breaking the bottle?

27

"Be realistic, PLAN for a miracle." Osho

Now, since you are probably not a Zen monk, you may very well answer, "Who wants to get the stupid goose out of its bottle anyway?" Or, "Hey, to hell with the bottle, let's put the goose in the freezer and eat it for Thanksgiving."

Okay, I can see where you're coming from, but permit me to suggest that you may not be grasping all the implications of this deeply significant koan.

You see the goose symbolizes your consciousness, your free spirit, your ultimate reality; while the bottle represents your mind. In other words, this koan is saying that your consciousness is trapped inside the mental structures of your mind, and if you ever want to experience the ultimate freedom of pure consciousness, pure meditation, pure liberation, then you need to find a better answer to the question than serving up roast goose for dinner.

For example, let's take a look at the story of how Nansen, a very famous Zen Master, dealt with this question. The tale goes like this:

The official, Riko, once asked Nansen to explain to him the old problem of the goose in the bottle.

"If a man puts a gosling in the bottle," said Riko, "and feeds it until it is full-grown, how can the man get the goose out without killing it or breaking the bottle?"

Nansen gave a great clap with his hands and shouted, "Riko!"

"Yes, Master," said the official with a start.

"See," said Nansen, "The goose is out!"

When I first heard Osho tell this story, I got it – instant Zen.

28

My sister was wrong. My goose isn't cooked, my goose is out! For the longest time after this major spiritual realization I thought I was enlightened. It took me a while to realize that Osho is the one who is out, while Krishna Prem – that's me, Margie's brother – is back in the bottle every time I get my buttons pushed or strike "out" with the ladies. Osho is out. Most of the time, I am in. But I don't feel bad about it. I am in a love affair with my Master. And when I look into Osho and I see his freedom, I feel my own potential to be free – and sometimes get a taste of it, too.

On my most recent trip to America, my sister Margie and I drove back to the home we grew up in. We were both "big kids" by that time – our father had long ago left his body. As we pushed open the old screen door, I turned to Margie and asked with a smile, "If Mum were alive today, how do you think she'd feel about me meditating in India, so far away from home?" Margie laughed and said, "Your goose would be cooked." This time I had the right answer. I clapped my hands and shouted, "The goose is out." She gave me a kiss on my balding head and said, "Go back to India. You're crazy!"

Soon afterwards, Margie also left her body, struck down by cancer. Her last words to me were true to her never-to-be-surrendered role of big sister: "Grow up." Funnily enough, Osho's last words to me were, "It's not my responsibility that you get enlightened. It's your responsibility." This just goes to prove that elder sisters and Zen masters never give up – fortunately.

QUESTION: OSHO, YOU SAY THE GOOSE IS OUT ALREADY. WHY DOES IT FEEL SO IMPOSSIBLE TO GRASP?

"I believe in God. I just don't trust anybody who works for him."Bob Ekant Pochter

"Because it is already out! Just see the point, don't think about it. A moment's thought, and you have gone far away. Don't brood about it, just see it. It is not a question of thinking about and about, going in circles, it is not a question of great intellectuality, of philosophical acumen, of logical efficiency. It is not a question of a trained mind; it is a question of an innocent heart.

Just see it! Wipe your eyes of all the tears, wipe your eyes of all the dust that has accumulated on them, and just look at existence. A leaf falling from the tree may become your enlightenment."

Osho

As I grew up, I realized I gave up playing sports mainly because I simply forgot how to "play." My brother Brian reminded me one day of our childhood motto: the brother who has the most fun wins. In that way there is a very good chance that everyone wins. At that moment, well into my forties, I took up the game of tennis, or as we call it at the Osho Meditation Resort, Zennis, the inner game of tennis. However, shit happens and one day, I complained to my friend, "My tennis elbow really hurts. I guess I should see a doctor." My friend said, "Don't do that. There's a computer at the drug store that can diagnose anything quicker and cheaper than a doctor. Simply put in a sample of urine, and the computer will diagnose your problem and tell you what you can do about it. And it only costs ten dollars."

I figured I had nothing to lose, so I filled a jar with a urine sample and went to the drug store. Finding the computer, I poured in the sample and deposited the ten dollars. The computer started making some noise and various lights started flashing. After a brief pause, out popped a small slip of paper, which said the following: "You have tennis elbow. Soak your arm in warm

"Ninety-nine percent of your nightmares never come true. Do not live in fear

water, avoid heavy labor. It will be better in two weeks." That evening while thinking how amazing this new technology was and how it would change medical science forever, I began to wonder if this computer could be fooled. I decided to give it a try. I mixed together some tap water, a stool sample from my dog, and urine samples from my wife and daughter. To top it off, I masturbated into the concoction. I went back to the drug store, located the computer, poured in the mixture and deposited the ten dollars. The machine again made the usual noises, flashed its lights, and printed out the following analysis:

"Your tap water is too hard. Get a water softener. Your dog has ringworm. Bathe him with anti-fungal shampoo. Your daughter is using drugs. Put her in a rehabilitation clinic. Your wife is pregnant with twin girls. They aren't yours. Get a lawyer.
And if you don't stop jerking off, your elbow will never get better."

"The ego can exist only if you take yourself and everything seriously. Nothing kills the ego like playfulness, like laughter. When you start taking life as fun, the ego has to die, it cannot exist anymore. Ego is illness; it needs an atmosphere of sadness to exist. Seriousness creates the sadness in you. Sadness is a necessary soil for the ego."

Osho

Atisha's Heart Meditation

I am well aware that I am writing a light-hearted look at life at a trying time in our lives. I often ask myself if our small planet is at its most violent peak or is that I have simply become acutely aware of man's inhumanity to man. When I am down, I often call upon

and miss the joy life has in store." Dr. Brian Alman

this simple meditation as my sword of awareness. Thank you Atisha for bringing miracles to my miseries.

This is how Osho brought Atisha into my consciousness; "Let me remind you, in the last sutra Atisha was saying that when you take the breath in, let it become your meditation that all the suffering of all the beings in the world is riding on that incoming breath and reaching your heart. Absorb all that suffering, pain and misery in your heart, and see a miracle happen."

You are cordially invited to do this alchemical meditation every day for the rest of your life.

"To wish you were someone else is to waste the person you are." Sven Goran Eriksson

Chapter 2

Courage: The Joy of Living Dangerously

"Aloneness simply means completeness. You are whole; there is no need of anybody else to complete you. So try to find out your innermost center where you are always alone, have always been alone. In life, in death – wherever you are – you will be alone. But it is so full! It is not empty; it is so full and so complete and so overflowing with all the juices of life, with all the beauties and benedictions of existence, that once you have tasted your aloneness, the pain in the heart will disappear. Instead, a new rhythm of tremendous sweetness, peace, joy, bliss, will be there."

The Path of the Mystic, Osho

My master once told me, and I love it, "My head on my shoulders is a great idea. My head on your shoulders is a very bad idea." In other words, whatever I say is for me and needs to be lived by me, and doesn't automatically apply to you. I'm sharing this with you because I've been round the block a few times and I've picked up some useful insights into life, which may help you along the way and save you some time! But it's up to you to decide whether to pick up and play with what I say or throw it away. Go on, try my shoes on and take a walk in them! Even if they're not your size, they're not gonna ruin your feet! Play with these ideas and find out which ones work and which ones don't! Surely, some sixty-year-old dude who's spent thirty years in India must have something useful to say?

But decide for yourself what's good for you. Don't rely on me or others to tell you what to do. Respond to your own life and go

Sign on the door of a meditation center: Out of body. Back in twenty minutes.

with what you feel attracted to, regardless of how crazy it may seem! I think it was Buddha who said, "Be a light unto yourself," and I know it was Osho who said, "Be a joke unto yourself!" Following your own light and taking responsibility is the way to go.

That reminds me of a beautiful Sufi story. It's about a gentleman who is praying to God and while he is praying to God his camel runs away. So he complains to God, "Look, here I am praying to you and my camel runs away." And God replied, "So tie up your camel first and then pray!" In other words, don't blame me for your actions and choices; take responsibility for your own life. I can't live your life for you; you can't live your life for me. We all have to tie up our own camels!

That's enough about me, what about you? What's your story, morning glory? C'mon, everyone has a story! Probably it runs along similar lines as mine; born in nineteen hundred and something, raised in Marblehead, Massachusetts, went to Gremlin High, loved baseball, hated math, got laid, got a job, got married... and so on and so forth. Well that's just the basic outline. Add to that all your individual good- and bad-luck stories, your dramas, fascinating coincidences and passionate encounters, and you too have a unique and incredible tale to tell.

And like me, you've probably told your story a gazillion times or so at least, mainly to unsuspecting victims at parties. And like me, you have probably spiced up your story a bit, by adding in a few extra details here and taking out a few extra details there, just to make it more exciting and entertaining. Don't worry, we all do it!

34

And, I used to compare my story with other people's stories and I used to think, "My god, poor Michael!" until I realized that it's not like everyone else had the same warm, fuzzy story apart from me. Sure, we all get a different kick-start in life; some of us get off the blocks smoothly and some of us trip over at the starting line! We're all having different experiences and leading different lives. There isn't a normal person, normal family or normal life out there. Everyone's life journey is totally unique! Even identical twins, born of the same egg, brought up by the same parents in the same family, in the same home, have different perspectives, experiences, stories and lives, and if you really get close, they even have slightly different appearances too. I guess we're all a little odd....

An elephant asks a camel, "Why are your breasts on your back?"

"Well," says the camel, "I think that's a bit of a strange question coming from someone whose dick is on his face!"

But ultimately whether our life stories are different or the same doesn't really matter. The question is, is my life-story me? Is your life story you? I mean, isn't that on-going tale we tell and update each year really just data we have gathered together about ourselves? And if that's the case, then who am I? And who are you?

Have you ever stopped to question who you really are? What did you come up with? Some definite ideas, vague feelings or maybe just some good old plain "don't knows?" You know, there's nothing wrong with "don't knows". In fact, "don't know" is a really a great place to start, because when you already think you know, you're not open to learning anything new. When you've

awareness is freedom." Krishnamurti

already got it all figured out, no one can tell you anything. And when you already think you know who you are, you're not open to searching for the true U. I like that line, "Those of you who think you know piss off those of us who do!"

So anyway, "don't knows" are great. I know they always get a bad press out in the world, because doubt, especially self-doubt, isn't the in-thing at all, what with everyone out there raving on about self-confidence, self-worth and self-esteem! But look at it again! A doubt is just a question. Doubting is just inquiring, which in terms of searching for U is really healthy and useful. In fact, doubt or enquiry is what the whole scientific process is built on. Science basically enquires and enquires until it finds out what's true. And as much as we might think the search is all about trusting, trusting, trusting, which is certainly part of it; it does in fact involve a lot of questioning, enquiring and investigating. It begins with a seed of doubt in our mind, with a nagging question, whether it is, "Who am I?" or "What am I doing here?" or "What is true?" I heard Osho say, "Do not repress doubt, but go into it, doubt, doubt, doubt until you find the indubitable!"

"Who do you think you are?" Sounds rude doesn't it? Probably because we imagine some big woman with her hands on her hips shouting it out in a frighteningly loud voice. But what I'm trying to get at here is that when we ask that question, what thoughts spring to mind? "I'm a man," "I'm a woman," "I'm nice," "I'm wicked," "I'm sexy!" The point is that whatever we come up with comes from our mind and our thinking. We use our minds to define who we are. We think, analyze, imagine and invent who we are, rather than putting our thoughts aside and seeing who is already there.

See, there's a big difference between thinking and knowing who we are. Thinking involves actively using the mind and having

"This life our celebration of the joys we've come to know. My love for you,

thoughts, while knowing involves putting the mind aside and having no thoughts. How can I explain it? I guess it's the difference between thinking about the taste of coffee and actually tasting it. Say for example you've never tasted coffee before. You could try and imagine what it tastes like, from the smell of it or the look of it, or you could ask someone to try and describe it to you. However, imagining the flavor is just not the same as putting your lips to the liquid and actually tasting it.

In a nutshell, thinking about who you are isn't the same as knowing who you are, and when you know who you are, you just can't describe it to anybody, you can only hint and point and hope. So, before U can know U, we first need to take a peek at who you think you are.

When someone asks us, "Who are you?" what do we say? I guess to some degree it depends on the circumstances. I mean, we're someone's friend if it gets us in the door and we're not someone's friend if it keeps us out. We're Joe's brother if Joe is a super-cool guy and we don't even know Joe if he's a total idiot! We chop and change our story depending on what works for us at the time. It's normal, sexy and fun. Everyone does it.

But generally when someone asks us, "Who are you?" nine times out of ten we just say our name. We automatically come out with, "I'm John," "I'm Jim," or "I'm Jane," or "My name is Zoe and this is my brother Xavier" My god, it's like we're on autopilot. It's out of our mouths before we've even thought about it, because it's what we've been taught to believe and trained to say. It's like when someone asks, "How are you?" We automatically reply "Fine, thank you," whether we are or not. And it's the same when an interviewer says, "So, tell me about yourself," and we reply, "Well, I'm twenty years old and I went to school at da-di-da and I

Osho, is overflowing." Milarepa

graduated in '06…" and then we whittle on about what we've done and how perfect we are for the job while the interviewer just sits back and yawns.

And it's OK! It's what we're expected to do in social situations, respond normally like other people. Our name and where we're from is our bus ticket into society. I mean it just doesn't look good if someone asks us who we are or how we're doing, and we answer, "Hmm, well, er, I don't really know." But in some ways it would be more honest! The point is, that just as "I'm fine thank you" isn't the real answer to the question "How are you?" so "I'm Giovanni Francesco from Milano," isn't the real answer to the question "Who am I?"

Maybe one way to look at it is to see when you are miserable, how much time do you have on your hands? And when you are happy, how quickly time flies? Sometimes Osho used to say to me, "Why don't you write a little song about all the happy moments?" It is difficult to remember joy because it disappears in that very moment. So kind of go back into your life, and take those ten or twelve moments when you were ecstatic, and write a song. It will not be a long song. If I ask you to write a miserable song, I will just fall asleep listening to you just going on and on about how shitty life had treated you. And life treats you shitty when you are not yourself, when you are trying to live up to what people and your personality expect of you. Joy is when life is happening. It's a celebration.

Just yesterday I went out for lunch. I went on the bicycle and the gentleman that I was having lunch with was driving a car. And often times in the city, like in Amsterdam, the boy on the bike gets there first. And I went to the restaurant and I sat at the table that was reserved for us. And the waiter was being a waiter. And I said

"Right now I'm having amnesia and déjà vu at the same time - I think I've

to him, "I don't need a waiter right now, I'm going to wait for my friend. Could you possibly just relax?" And he said, "It's my job to be a waiter." And I said, "I understand, I understand... tell me one thing, when you go home tonight, who are you?" And he said, "When I go home today, I'm going to be a father to my one-year-old son." I said, "Well, that is really great. So during the day you're wearing a hat called "I'm being a waiter." And at night you're wearing a hat called "I'm being a father." Well, I just want to say one thing, there is a moment when you have to take off your waiter-hat, and put on your father-hat. And in that moment, you are naked. In that moment, you are simply you. So I want you to be aware that in that moment, you are not a waiter, you are not a father, you are only you. And then when you greet your son, as his father, you'll feel freshness, because you also know that you are you first and a father second. You are you first and you are a waiter second. So right now I don't need a waiter. Is it possible for you to be naked? Is it possible for you to just treat me like a human being?" And it was so cute, maybe it was an unconscious thing on his part, but he actually just sat down on a chair beside me. I think he was so amazed that I was asking him to be himself, he relaxed so much that he was sitting down next to me. And cutely I got a little nervous. Who is this guy sitting next to me as a human being? I can actually remember saying to myself, "My God, you are a waiter. Stand up and take care of me. Go and get me a glass of water. I can't handle being with another human being right now." I think in this situation the guy got my teaching, and it became real for him and it made me nervous.

Are superman and superwoman really fantasy? I think we're all superheroes really. We're all switching roles and characters throughout the day. We're all striving to be different things to different people, or worse still, trying to be all things to all people.

forgotten this before." Steven Wright

With one swish of our cape we can suddenly morph into someone else, and beneath our undoubtedly sexy superhero outfits, we're all just actors in the play of life.

Coming to know the true you is really very, very simple. It's just about taking off all those hats, all those titles, stories and labels you've pinned on yourself. I call this getting naked, getting out of your own way. How much energy do we waste trying to play the efficient boss, the faithful husband, the playful father, the dutiful son and the loyal friend? How much energy could we save by tossing the hatbox away and just being ourselves? Sure, it's fun to act, to put on different masks and play different roles, but when do we get to really relax? Only when we sit down for that gin and tonic?

So these things can happen… this is a great meditation. Hats. I call it hats. Just notice which hat you are wearing now. I am a boss. I am a student. I am a mother. I am a wife, I am a lover, I am a joker, and I'm a midnight toker. And watch how many roles you play every day, in every way. And just remember to look for yourself as you put one hat on and take another hat off. Or, if you can do it as many multitasking people on planet earth do, they put one hat on top of another without ever taking the first hat off. This is very, very confusing and you probably don't recognize this because you are probably my boss. You know, the higher you are up on the society scale, probably means you learned the art of putting on the second hat without taking off the first hat.

And conversely it can be called peeling the onion. Taking off one hat after another, saying this is not who I am, this hat is not who I am. This job is not who I am. This religion is not who I am. You can keep peeling the onion, peeling the onion, peeling the onion until you get back to I am. I exist. I am alive. And you can

Graffiti on a wall: God is dead! (Signed Friedrich Nietzsche)

take this all the way back to I am not a man. I am not a woman. You can go all the way back to I am existence.

Now, the problem with "I am existence," is that it's just simply not a knowing. It's a not-knowing. It's I am neither a boss, I am neither a wife, I am neither a Jew, I am neither a Christian. It's a not-knowing. And I just want to suggest to you, that a lot of people, or at least the me I am talking about, have real fear of being naked; fear of not being my conditioning, of not being my personality, of not being a boss, or an employee. In other words, I am asking you to take away your identities, all of them, until you are absolutely naked, until you are not even a man or a woman. Can you imagine that? Can you imagine not being your sex? Just innocent and naked.

So it is a question of not knowing who you are instead of knowing who you are. In the East we often say not knowing is the most intimate experience you can have; breathing in and out without being a personality, without being a society. Can you imagine that? Just breathing in and breathing out, breathing in and breathing out without an identity. It's a miracle.

What I'm trying to say is that the truth is not from the East. It is not created by meditation in India. It is everywhere. The truth is I don't mean to divide the East and the West. I don't mean to say that the East is enlightened and the West is asleep. It is not the case. There is truth, and truth only. There is no East and there is no West when it comes to truth.

There is something about being in India that says: give it up. Sit here. Be. Let the sun set. Don't define it. Just be. And there is something about in the West: we are always describing the moment, and talking about the moment, and killing the moment.

Graffiti below that: Friedrich Nietzsche is dead! (Signed God)

There is something about the West that wants to make the moment a material thing.

So my experience of living in the East was that of meditation. And my experience of living in the West was to afford to live. However, that is just a thought. Has nothing to do with reality. In reality it is great to meditate and there is nothing wrong with paying the rent. So maybe the West has taught the material truth and the East has taught the spiritual truth. But in fact my experience is that if you are materially well off and you don't have a spiritual life, you are a poor man. And I honestly have come to the feeling that if you pray and meditate all the time, and can't afford the rent, I don't think that is such a great situation either. My feeling is slipping and sliding; taking care of your inner life, taking care of your outer life. That to me is joy. I like it.

The old expression on the Jewish napkin at the Bar Mitzvah: I would rather be rich and healthy than poor and sick. On the other napkin: you can never be too rich or too thin. Those expressions help us to laugh at ourselves. That is what really works: laughing at ourselves. Breaking us down until we can slip and slide between "I am existence" and "I enjoy the good life" also. As Osho is famously remembered for saying, "I am a simple man. I simply like the best of everything."

In the same way in reality there is not an East and a West. In reality there is not a big you that is existence and a little you that is a personality. There is only you. But for the sake of writing a book and having some fun, I have divided you in two.

Language itself is simply a division. First there was the word. No, first there was silence. And out of that silence comes the joy of communication, the joy of sharing what is actually going on now. So, first there is not a big you and a little you, there is only you.

Mahatma Gandhi: "I think it would be a good idea." (When asked what he

But language itself, as soon as I speak, I am coming out of silence to make noise. And as soon as you do that, it is just simply what we can call a division; a division between the big you and the little you, between the East and the West, between silence and the spoken word. So I am just going to take my best shot and you try it on and see if it works for you. If it doesn't work for you, you have wasted some money. It is ok, you can probably sell it to somebody else because just as many people are interested in being naked as in wearing an Armani suit. So if you are in an Armani suit and you had bought this book by accident, just go out and look for somebody naked and sell or give him the book. It is not a big deal.

So one time in Amsterdam I had a couple of Duval beers. It is a Belgian beer and god, you get drunk by those Belgian beers! I understand that those beers were created by monks in Belgium during the wintertime way back. While these guys know how to pray, they know how to make a good beer! It is very, very strong. Anyway, I had a few beers, and there I am standing at the canal between two parked cars, full of liquid. And I know you are not supposed to do it, but nobody was watching and it was dark and I took a pee. And anybody that is drunk, especially if they are not drunk that often, ends up peeing in the canal for the very first time, your ego is such that you might think that the canal might overflow. Anyway, after I had released myself with a sense of satisfaction, I looked across the other side of the canal and there is Osho. And I said, "Osho!" It was kind of funny and I must've been really drunk, because you know Osho is no longer in his body. I said, "Osho, how do I get to the other side?" And he hollered back to me, at least I heard him holler back to me, "You are on the other side!"

There are not even two sides to a canal, in a sense. Often times we just divide things until it is untrue, for example our minds, our

43

thought about Western civilization)

hearts and our spirits. We tend to feel that they are separate and fighting in trying to get our attention. When in fact the deeper you go into who you are, the more there is only one left. So the head and the heart were actually good friends until they met us and we separated them and put them in separate corners and said, "You guys can't get along." And by the way, I want to give you the best example of meditation I have ever heard, and that is that we are built like a thermometer. You know, we have lots and lots of energy in our belly. And this energy flows upward to our heart and into our minds. Our mind is actually the smallest part of the thermometer of life. But what happened somehow to me, and maybe to you also, is that I began to not be able to trust this. And I just started trying to keep as much energy in my head as possible. I even put on a tie and I tied the tie really tight, so this energy in my head is what I had shared with other people. This energy in my head, which was cut off by my tie, no longer had heart and no longer had a belly. And it got very, very stale. Then I just loosened my tie and fell back down into my heart and into my belly. And I think when you begin from the head, you just never feel grounded.

My idea of meditation is that you trust your instincts, you trust your belly. And this energy moves up to express itself and it comes through the heart, which is very, very loving, and then into the mind that is you. That feels right to you. Not what you have been taught but what you are feeling in this very moment. This very moment is it. This is it, so kind of see yourself as a thermometer. You are in your belly, in your gut. Expressing through the heart comes out of your mouth, through your mind, and it is a duet. It is oneness. It is who you are. You may piss-off the guy next to you and that may be rough. He may be so shocked by someone speaking his own truth that that pissed-off immediately brings him

44

to who he is. He will stare back and we shall have an exciting conversation.

So try it. Do not come up with readymade answers, do not come up with readymade feelings, and do not come up with readymade truth. Sit. Come from right now, through your body, through your heart, to your mind, and express yourself. This is what they call the here and now. It will be dangerous by the way, but exciting, so let's give it a try.

Maybe a simpler way of saying it is that I was having a cup of coffee with a woman friend of mine, who was just into the art of meditation. And I asked, "Could you give me an example of how meditation has changed your life?" And she said, "You know, I used to be very cool on the outside. I know I'm a good-looking woman, and I know I am going to have fun, and I would just be cool, very cool on the outside, because I knew life was coming to visit me in the form of boys. But I always ended up totally boiling, totally pissed-off on the inside. And these poor guys never knew what had hit them. And I never got into a relationship because the outer package is this cool very beautiful woman to a lot of men. But when they actually found out who they were dating, they would run away just as fast, if not faster as they were running towards me in the first place. Once I learned the art of meditation, I became just the opposite. I was totally cool on the inside, and what you got on the outside, was brand new and refreshing and wild and honest. I never knew what I was going to say or how I was going to react, or how I was going to act for that matter. But I found it much more honest. And when I did date a man for example, he knew what he was getting into. He had the guts to ask me out. And I had the honesty to say yes or no."

45

I found it very refreshing, her example. It is great to be just who you are inside-out. You don't know how life is going to happen to you right now. But I'd rather be honest and open and wild than conditioned; knowing what I'm going to say before I say it, and doing the right thing every moment as I was taught.

I was sitting before Osho once upon a time. I don't know, about ten or twelve of us were in the room, so I don't know if he was talking to me directly or to somebody else. It does not really make a difference because if I had heard it, he was talking to me. He was saying it is easy to be strong and invulnerable. It is easy to be weak and vulnerable. The real life question is, "Can you be strong and vulnerable?" This question rocked my world from then until now.

Everybody is in the game together. Everybody has a right to be here. Everybody is right. How is that for an expression? Everybody is right. I am right, you are right. That does not mean that I want to have lunch with you by the way. I might not like your rightness. But how you are acting and what you are doing is right for you.

It's very, very simple and I hate it. But let us just say that I am a man and I am ready to be an American. Well, that is right. But what is wrong in my opinion is to be an American and to put my thoughts and conditioning on top of a rack and say, "Wouldn't you like to be like me?" I am right for who I am and so are you right for who you are. Does not make us necessarily friends, but it may give us the space for everybody to work through their conditioning and into themselves. And I trust from my belly that that kind of an experience is unconditional love and acceptance, that there is enough space for the two of us. When I can allow myself to be, and allow you to be also, that is a very peaceful situation.

"Freedom from the past means the freedom to create a life of presence, love

War for me is when two people are right and they feel the other person is wrong. Peace for me is when two people are right and they allow each other to be.

Again, my head on my shoulders: great idea! My head on your shoulders: bad idea! Simplistic: yes. True: maybe. It is up to you, for me it is true.

Jesus is said to have said, "Thou shalt not judge," I think if you look into your own mind you will see that's all your mind knows how to do, judge, judge, judge. What he meant is you may be able to judge an act; someone robs a bank and your money is in that bank, you are gonna be pretty upset, and you can judge the man for his act so you can put him in jail for a few years so he learns what the difference is between right and wrong, but you can't judge him. We simply can't judge each other. We don't know enough.

And what we do know is not who we are but how we feel, how we judge others. In fact this shows that it's true that the mind is simply a prison, that when the mind runs our life that we are in prison and of course we can decorate this mind, we can build a beautiful house in our mind, we can put beautiful furniture in our mind, we can put a Mercedes Benz in our mind, the mind is a pretty big area and you can do whatever you want. But in the end, if you are not the witness watching your mind, your mind is going to own you. You will never be able to separate from your mind, even for a moment. So basically what we are doing all day long is trading in our Mercedes Benz or our Rolls Royce, but we are always identified with our possessions and our thoughts and our feelings. What meditation teaches us is not that we should not have a Mercedes, but that if we have a Mercedes it's simply a car. Our car, our mind is simply not who we are.

and responsibility." Tarika

Basically what I am saying is that our mind is telling us "we want this car, we want a future, we want a relationship," because the mind is saying "as long as you do what I want, we are going to succeed in this lifetime." And so what we never find out is that without a mind we still want everything, we still want the good life, we still want to experiment, we still want to make the same mistake once. So the first thing to be understood is that your mind is never going to agree to meditate because the mind wants to be the boss. And what I would like to say is if you meditate, you will be able to use the mind instead of the mind using you. Now of course the mind is a product of society and a product of religion and basically a product of your parents.

Let me ask you this question: What is your earliest memory? I came upon this question when a boy was in the meditation group that I was leading and he said, "You know, if I knew that this day was going to be about meditation I would not have come to the group." I was leading one day out of five days. One day was re-birthing and one day was based on family constellation and my day was based on meditation. He made this comment and I said, "You know it really doesn't make a difference to me whether you are here or not, if I were you I would leave. Why be somewhere where you don't wanna be? We are probably not gonna have such good time together." And he said, "Well, talk me into it." So very simply I used this example. I said, "What was your earliest memory?" and he said, "My earliest memory was age three…" and he began to smile because it was a pleasant memory. For many of us, our earliest memory isn't pleasant, it's when we hear the word "no" for the very first time and understand that we are not getting our own way. But in this case he had a happy first memory. I said, "Great, you remember everything from age three on so tell me how you are gonna die?" He looked at me and he said, "I don't know how I am

"A free man belongs to himself and nobody else. A free man is simply an energy

going to die." So what I said to him basically was, "Let's call your life a book. Let's say you are not a human being, you are actually a novel. You begin this novel at page three. You don't know what happened before page three and you don't know how this novel is going to end. So I agree with you that nothing may happen today and in fact nothing does happen in meditation that is successful as such, but if I were you, I might stay for the whole day, because you don't like meditation, because we are planting seeds today, because I say, and I can't prove it to you and I can't even say that I know it myself, that life began for you before your parents made love. And life will go on after you leave this body of yours. In other words there is a part of you that is eternal and there is a part of you that comes and goes and what we learn in meditation when we look into ourselves is 'I am not my body.'" Now this is a pretty revolutionary thought and I am not asking you to believe me. Maybe in the course of reading this book we both get clear, I am not writing a book about knowing, I am writing a book about not knowing. In the East we often say not knowing is the most intimate experience. What we learn in meditation is that not knowing is absolutely a delight, that life is not a problem to be solved. Life is a mystery to be lived.

It felt good when the young man stayed for the day of meditation and at the end of the day I said to him, "You know, my earliest memory was also age three." We had a good chuckle because I said, "What we are doing here today is planting seeds, doing different kinds of meditations that someday you may say, "Wow, I am going to go back to that seed and see if it's grown, I am going to water that seed by doing the meditation again." I don't know what I wanna say right now; meditation is simply a way to get out of our own way. I often wonder when I speak about meditation if I am not encouraging people to quit work and quit

with no name, no form, no race, no nation." Osho

their relationship and come to the East, to be a drop-out. No, that's not what I am trying to say, there is a vertical line, there is a horizontal line and the two lines cross. Jesus' gift to us of the symbol of the cross is a beautiful way to express meditation as I am speaking about it now. There is a vertical line where we take care of ourselves as best as we can without hurting anyone else. Very often in meditation what we say is that if you were born to be a dancer, you still go to a dance school and you become a dancer. If you were born to become a doctor, you still go to medical school to become a doctor. It seems like there is always a seed, there is always a passion in you and it needs to be watered, it needs to be educated, it needs experience in order to come to fruition. And there is a horizontal line which is just the fact that you are spirit, the fact that you are alive, the fact that you are a human being, not only a human doer that was born to be a doctor and goes to medical school but actually a spirit that you have come here to be. And those two lines cross and when they cross, and again when you are not in your own way, when you are responding to your own passion, when you are feeling life and you are feeling rich, there is no horizontal and there is no vertical, there is only the here and the now.

So in a sense this book is just the opposite of any book you have ever read. In other words you won't read this book and become a doctor but if you were a doctor you may begin to get undressed, you may begin to get naked. We call this peeling the layers of the onion and you peel one more thought, one more conditioning, one more religion, you keep peeling back and back and back and instead of getting dressed up you dress down. You just become naked before existence and the cosmic joke is that you are you. That you can't take yourself away from who you are but you can continue to put on things that don't fit, put on jobs that

"Aum Mani Padme Hum." Ancient Buddhist Chant

don't make sense, marry the wrong woman. I don't know, we just continue to do the wrong thing because we are not coming from who we are as much as we are coming from who others want us to be. So let's get naked, it's up to you it's up to me. You will recognize yourself and I will recognize myself.

What we are talking about is a technique from the East that is called witnessing. What we wanna do is watch ourselves. I watch me, you watch you. I am not gonna watch you, you are not gonna watch me. It's difficult at first. But let's put it this way, just go inside your mind and just begin to watch it, is it my mind or can I see my mind? Is it my feelings or can I witness my feelings? For example, I ask you who you are and most people that I meet in America always tell me their name. I say, "No, no, no, that's not what I wanna know." And then they might tell me what they do for a living, or which religion they belong to. I say, "No, no, no. that's not who you are, is it?" Is that who we are? So basically you ask yourself who you are and it will take some time before you can strip away that which has been given to you from the very beginning of your life here on planet earth. You probably started at the nine months in the womb when your parents began your education into how you should act in society in order to get along. How to trust, how not to trust, what you are wanting to do when you grow up, what school you are going to go to. You are absolutely Jewish, you are absolutely Christian, please marry a Jewish girl, please marry a Christian girl, please marry a Protestant girl, whatever conditioning your parents force-fed you with. This conditioning is still in you. In fact as long as this conditioning exists, you are not you. You are not G.U.R.U…. Your parents will do all of this as they want the best for you; they literally steal your life away from you and try to impose their reality, with the best of intentions. They want you to be like they want you to be and of

51

course it's very painful to look at the mind and find out that actually you are a product of your environment, that you are not at all a clear, brand new, alive being. So when I ask who are, I don't want answers based on any of this, I want you to be as naked as possible, because when you're totally naked you are the truth. I would like to advertise your truth right now, because what you said to me, to my reading, is an expression of life: love yourself, and watch. Often we begin to meditate because we don't love ourselves. We begin to watch, we begin to witness, and we start throwing out all our conditioning, all these things we have just been talking about. Imagine if you look in the mirror right now and say to yourself, "My life up until this very moment has been, and is gonna continue to be, bullshit." You can get pretty depressed over that today if you don't have the tool of witnessing, the tool of meditation to get you through this. So at the same time as we are looking in a mirror saying, "I am bullshit," you might look at how thrilled you are to find that you are willing to drop your bullshit, drop the mind, be here and now, love yourself and watch.

This love word we are talking about now is love of yourself, so before you go on sharing with everyone what a great thing you did by reading a book on meditation and becoming the witness and accepting your bullshit, begin with yourself. Don't share anything unless it's out of love. It's a very selfish thing, meditation. I think one of the reasons it's so difficult for us in the West to meditate because we are taught to be not selfish. We have been taught to share and to give and my god, how can you share if you don't feel good about yourself? Can you imagine what you are sharing when you don't love yourself? It's just the opposite with meditation. What we are saying is be completely selfish and out of this selfishness you begin to fall in love and as you fall in love, there is no one to love. There is no you, you begin to see that you are

52

"Understanding is not of the mind: understanding is of the heart. You will have silence, you are bliss and as you come more from silence, your actions are neither right nor wrong, neither left nor right, they are just coming and you are just sharing and you begin to love the other for who they are because they are in the same movie you are in, they are human beings and they may be totally dressed in conditioning still. You may have just dropped your concept of religion, yet you can't expect everybody else at that very same moment to drop their sense of religion.

And you know this feeling when you become naked; you begin to love everyone for who they are. So out of this selfishness, out of this desire to be honest and true to yourself, the self tends to fall away. And when you come out from this space, it's called compassion. You start to see that other people are in the very own process; they are doing their best to get through this day. The only difference is that you are beginning to wake up and as you begin to wake up you don't shit on the people that are still asleep. You have compassion for them and you just have a little prayer saying, "My god, I hope they go inside; that they are willing to wake up, that they are willing not to lay their life on everyone they meet."

I told you the story about "This too shall pass." Everything is coming and going, your body is coming and going, your thoughts are coming and going, your life is coming and going. There is nothing you can hold on to. I think it came a lot through the hippie generations in America that change is the only thing that's permanent. So this king meditated on "This too shall pass" and it's one of the things that I meditate on sometimes in my own life, because we always want to fall in love forever and the only thing I wanna say about relationship is that this too will pass. And it's spelled TWO. All relationships are here to teach us, all relationships are here to pass. So I know that when you read a book about meditation, you are always praying for a miracle. You are

53

to fall in love." Osho

always saying if I read this book my relationship will work and I will live happily ever after with my beloved. In fact it may be true, but I haven't seen many examples in the East, in the West, in my bed, or in my mind. Relationships seem to come and go. It does not mean that they are not worth it; it does not mean that they don't teach you something, but please don't own your wife, please don't own your child. Love is a space; you can learn a lot from love, and that risk is always available to us and it gives life color and fulfillment. But let's get it for once and for all: there is no such thing as a soulmate, there is no such thing at all. I don't know if I am really just coming from my own terrible love life or from my own great times in love. But it feels to me to be the truth, this two will pass and I am ready right now to be in love forever.

At this point I put all my awareness into this one massive sailboat crossing the horizon, crossing just in front of the sunset, and in that very moment I became ecstatic. I have never been so happy in all my life; it was almost like "I" did it. It's probably like when a little child looks at his shit and says, "What a creation!" Have you ever seen a little three year-old looking at his own shit and saying, "I created that?" Well, that's how I felt with this massive sailboat in front of the sunset. I became ecstatic to the point where I disappeared. I disappeared from this known body, which I had been living in for thirty years; I was just hanging out in existence. Quite a feeling, quite an experience, in this very moment I was not the body, I was not the mind, I was just a presence. I hung out for a while until my mind came back and said, "What the fuck is going on with you?" And as soon as my mind reminded me that this was an "unnatural act" I got really scared and I screamed and I came back into my body and I just looked at the sky and I just started to scream at the heavens. I said to god for the very first time, "What the fuck just happened to me? This is a

54

dirty trick; I am not ready for this." I said, "I wanna meet a man just like the one who wrote this book, I know for a fact that you are not going to talk to me. I know that you are not going to come down and play with me because you never have, and the first time I have ever experienced you it feels naughty. It feels like you pulled a dirty trick on me. So I need to meet a teacher, a guru, a master, whatever it's called. I need to be able to relate to you through a living human being." Now when you are in India and you start screaming at the sky, it's very easy to have your first disciples. I was surrounded by my fishermen friends, who I would help pull their boats up the beach after dark. They would always offer me a few fish in return and I would just giggle because I was a vegetarian by now. They were very sweet but now they were seeing something in me that I wasn't seeing in myself. In India it's very close; being a mad man and being a meditator is very close. I don't know if you know this but often when someone gets enlightened they don't invite you for a cup of tea, they immediately go into one of those deep silences which are so available in India. Or they enter a mad house where there are no locks on the doors and they begin to relate with the mad people because basically they are the only ones that wanna talk to them. Mad people are the only ones that understand them. The difference between a mad man and an enlightened being is that the mad man does not have the consciousness and the awareness and the guts to be himself. He had just gotten his mind to the point where it's easier for him to check out than to be present. That's about the only difference, and it's not really a big difference.

So here I am again in my known body, in my known mind and I am just completely upset. My fishermen friends really enjoyed seeing me scream at the sky and afterwards they walked me into the water and they just splashed water on me to take all the sand off my body and to cool me off, because I was feeling very hot. They were enjoying what they were doing, and the strength in their bodies when they moved me into the water was amazing. These little guys, these fishermen, every night and every morning pushed their very heavy boats in and out of the sea and you can see that they push from the ground up. When I was helping them to push, I was pushing from the waist up. I think a lot of Americans like myself are very strong from the waist up, big arms and big chest, but in this part of the world it's the other way round and they push from the very earth itself. It's a bit like the difference between a soccer player in Europe and football player in America. They were extremely loving and gentle towards me, treating me almost as if it had already happened to them or to a friend to theirs; they weren't even surprised that this tirade of words and this madness that was coming out of my mouth, insisting that god "help me right now in my hour of need." They showed tremendous respect for madness. I was simply pissed off that god pulled such a dirty trick on me.

It's the kind of moment in time where you no longer have a past that you could identify with; that you don't know what is going to happen in the future. You are so in the moment, it's so brand new; it's so spontaneous that it's complete unto itself. And funnily enough it wasn't really that big a deal. In fact I never really shared this story before. It was just a happening and it was a newness that did not feel new, and I felt I could not explain it. I felt it was too intimate to talk about and if I did bring up the subject with a lover or a friend, often times they looked me like I was just bonkers. So it has taken until now where I feel fine with what happened, that it now feels natural. And I am waiting for it to happen again. I bring this up because many years after I met Osho, I asked him, "Osho, I had an experience before I met you of disappearing, of not being the mind, of not being the body and to be honest with you, even

"Your task is not to seek for love, but merely to seek and find all the barriers

though I feel love for you, I would like this to happen again. How come it's not happening right now for example?" Osho said to me, "You know I understand that when it happened to you that you were in a sense a virgin, that you came unprotected into a moment, a brand new moment and this is how life can actually happen to you. And as you sit in front of me with your expectation and your desire for this to happen again, so that you can validate yourself as a meditator, all of this thought of meditation is keeping you from this experience of meditation. You need to come into this very moment as naked as you were in that moment. And it's not easy because the mind has a memory and it thinks if you do the same thing again that the same experience will happen again, and that is not what meditation is. And meditation cannot happen without being in the moment, being a child again with awareness."

Now you remember the book was written by Acharaya Rajneesh and I could not read the word Acharaya? I need just to say that when I met Osho and I fell in love with him, I did not mention this story to him. I felt it was between me and god and this gentleman that wrote Seeds of Revolutionary Thought. Basically what Osho said to me is if I don't regain my innocence I am gonna actually be more pissed off now at him and at myself than I was at god when I had the experience. It's gonna be more frustrating with the awareness that you can have an experience beyond the body mind, you are gonna be more upset now without having that experience. You are gonna get more and more frustrated. And this is why often times we do active meditations where we exhaust the body mind through dancing, through screaming, through letting-go. All of this is a preparation for lying down and relaxing and when I ask you to do these active meditations, it's so that when you finally do lie down to meditate, you don't fall asleep. Because often people when they lay down if they are not feeling alive, they

within yourself that you have built against it." Rumi

tend to go right to sleep. Oftentimes meditation is full awareness as the body relaxes; very similar to sleep, except in sleep often you check out and in meditation we tend to check in. We tend to remain here and now without the weight of the body, without the weight of the mind. Just in a free flow.

I hold the record for doing the one-hour Dynamic Meditation the most times in one day – twenty-four times to be exact. In the very early times with Osho this was his first and foremost active meditation, and just in case you are curious about how I knew I had done this meditation in my sleep, the answer is that I woke myself up screaming in the second stage. As I don't want you to consider this meditation technique lightly, I am including the exact instructions.

OSHO® DYNAMIC MEDITATION™

Recommended to be done in the morning, this hour-long method is a powerful way to kick-start your day. It provides an outlet for tension and withheld emotions as well as being a great energy-booster! Dynamic Meditation lasts one hour and is in five stages. It can be done alone, and will be even more powerful if it is done with others. It is an individual experience so you should remain oblivious of others around you and keep your eyes closed throughout, preferably using a blindfold. It is best to have an empty stomach and wear loose, comfortable clothing.

"This is a meditation in which you have to be continuously alert, conscious, aware, whatsoever you do. Remain a witness. Don't get

"To be in meditation is to be one. No confusion, no hesitation. A response, a

lost. While you are breathing you can forget. You can become one with the breathing so much that you can forget the witness. But then you miss the point.

"Breathe as fast as possible, as deep as possible; bring your total energy to it but still remain a witness. Observe what is happening as if you are just a spectator, as if the whole thing is happening to somebody else, as if the whole thing is happening in the body and the consciousness is just centered and looking.

"This witnessing has to be carried in all the three steps. And when everything stops, and in the fourth step you have become completely inactive, frozen, then this alertness will come to its peak."

Osho

First Stage: 10 minutes

Breathe chaotically through the nose, concentrating always on exhalation. The body will take care of the inhalation. The breath should move deeply into the lungs. Be as fast as you can in your breathing, making sure the breathing stays deep. Do this as fast and as hard as you possibly can – and then a little harder, until you literally become the breathing. Use your natural body movements to help you to build up your energy. Feel it building up, but don't let go during the first stage.

Second Stage: 10 minutes

Explode! Express everything that needs to be thrown out. Go totally mad. Scream, shout, cry, jump, shake, dance, sing, laugh; throw yourself around. Hold nothing back; keep your whole body moving. A little acting often helps to get you started. Never allow

natural attitude happens in every moment." Tishan

your mind to interfere with what is happening. Be total, be whole-hearted.

Third Stage: 10 minutes

With raised arms, jump up and down shouting the mantra, "Hoo! Hoo! Hoo!" as deeply as possible. Each time you land, on the flats of your feet, let the sound hammer deep into the sex center. Give all you have; exhaust yourself totally.

Fourth Stage: 15 minutes

Stop! Freeze wherever you are, in whatever position you find yourself. Don't arrange the body in any way. A cough, a movement – anything will dissipate the energy flow and the effort will be lost. Be a witness to everything that is happening to you.
Fifth Stage: 15 minutes

Celebrate through dance, expressing your gratitude towards the whole. Carry your happiness with you throughout the day.

If where you meditate prevents you from making a noise, you can do this silent alternative: Rather than throwing out the sounds, let the catharsis in the second stage take place entirely through bodily movements. In the third stage, the sound "Hoo" can be hammered silently inside.

You can download the music for this meditation or order the music on CD from www.osho.com

"The quality of your life is the quality of your relationships." Anthony Robbins

Chapter 3

Bliss: Living beyond Happiness and Misery

"There is no meaning in the world; all meaning is in the very center of your being. The world is simply noise, there is no music. Music is in the deepest recesses of your being – and that music has to be heard in all the noise of the world. Then the noise of the world functions as a backdrop, a background; it becomes a context. You can hear the inner music more clearly because of the noise. Then the noise is no longer a disturbance, rather a help. That's why I don't teach renunciation: I teach rejoicing."

The Dhammapada Vol 7, Osho

You're probably wondering how on earth I ended up with this name "Krishna Prem" and probably also wondering what it means! Well, it happened when I went to India and was sitting in front of Osho for the very first time. There I was, as dead as a door nail, at the feet of this living master, when I suddenly heard him say, "Would you like to take sannyas now?" Taking sannyas simply means being initiated into meditation. "Yes!" I replied and the next thing I heard him say was, "… and your new name will be Krishna Prem which means ecstasy and love." "Oh my god!" I thought, "I can't believe he's given me a name like Krishna!" What can I say? It's really funny how quickly a moment can turn from bliss to shit. So in the same instant as I was beginning to fall in love with my master, I was also beginning to hate my new name! "Krishna Prem." "Krishna Prem." I tried it on a few times but it was simply horrible and I vowed never to repeat this name to anyone ever again! It took me years to grow into my name, to like my name and to really understand it, that "Krishna" means one that attracts the divine, while "Prem" simply means love. My god, my name was

"Aum sweet aum." Advertising slogan for India Incredible India

such a big deal at the time, probably because I thought it said something about who I was. But now it doesn't matter if you call me Michael Mogul, Krishna Prem or just plain KP, like the English nuts, because it's ultimately not me!

So, what's in a name? Are you really John, Jim or Jane? Are you the same as all the other Johns, Jims and Janes you know? What happens if you change your name, does your personality suddenly change also? What about all those cutting nicknames you received at school? Were you really "Fatso" or "Dummy" or "Shitface?" Maybe Mr. P. Nut and his wife Hazel are really a sane couple? Maybe Dick Head is a really bright guy? What's in a name? Nothing!

If a master asks, "Who are you?" and you tell him your name is James, he will just laugh! He will laugh because he is not referring to your body, or your mind, or the label your parents gave you. He will laugh because he is asking, "Who were you before your parents made love?" "Who will you be after you no longer have a body?" and "Who is the you who is never born and never dies?" He will laugh because you have not begun to investigate your true identity, what is called in the East, your original face.

Our name is not who we are, it's just a convenient label we use to avoid going round saying, "Hey you!" all the time. It's simply a useful way of identifying a particular body and mind, and it's really useful in the world of admin! We're no more our name than we are our passport number, our Social Security number or our PIN (pain-in-the-neck) code!

It's funny, but when you ask someone who they are, maybe after they've told you their name, they tell you what they do for a

"A real friend is someone who walks in when the rest of the world walks out."

living. They might say, "I'm a tax officer" or "I'm a taxi driver" or even "I'm a taxidermist!" Here's a joke that says it all;

A guy is in the checkout line at a local supermarket, when he notices that the rather foxy blonde behind him has just raised her hand and smiled hello to him. He is rather surprised that such a stunner would be waving to him, and although she looks familiar, he can't quite place where he knows her from, so he asks her, "Sorry, do you know me?"

She replies "I may be mistaken, but I thought you might be the father of one of my children."

His mind shoots back to the one and only time he had been unfaithful.

"My god," he says, "Are you that stripper from my bachelor party that I fucked on the pool table in front of all my friends while your girlfriend whipped me with some wet celery and stuck a cucumber up my butt?"

"No," she replies, "I'm your son's English teacher."

See what I mean? Most of us spend so much time working, that we think our job, our profession, our latest promotion or demotion is who we are. Adults pass this idea of "we are what we do" onto us as kids, so as kids we then begin to think we are our good or bad school reports, our shiny trophies sitting on the mantelpiece or our confiscated toys. We learn to feel good about our achievements and bad about our failures, great about our wins and shitty about our losses!

If we're not identified with our job then we might be identified with our actions or behaviors, or even our habits or addictions. But just because we drink, smoke or sniff glue, doesn't mean that's

63

St. Francis of Assis

who we are. People say, "You are what you eat!" but that doesn't make us a cheese burger or a hot dog now does it? Just because we shout "fucking asshole" at the truck driver that nearly took our toes off, doesn't mean we're crass, or angry or bad. Just because we mind our p's and q's doesn't mean we're the most cultured person on the planet. Alternatively, maybe we think we're our kind or unkind acts; the dog we saved, the cat we ran over, the money we donated to charity or the bathrobe we stole from the hotel.

Jake was on his deathbed. His wife, Susan, was keeping vigil by his side. As she held his fragile hand, tears ran down her face. Her praying roused him from his slumber. He looked up and his pale lips began to move slightly.
"My darling Susan," he whispered.
"Hush, my love," she said, "Rest! Shhh! don't talk!"
He was insistent. "Susan," he said in his tired voice, "I have something I must confess to you."
"There's nothing to confess," replied the weeping Susan, "Everything's all right, go to sleep."
"No, no. I must die in peace, Susan. I slept with your sister, your best friend and your mother."
"I know," she replied, "That's why I poisoned you."

Now I'm not saying that what we do and say doesn't have consequences or effects in this world. For sure what we do and say shapes what we manifest in life. For sure we are responsible for our behaviors and actions, but are they who we are? There's so much emphasis in our society on doing, doing, doing, but when are we going to cut down on the doing and enjoy a little more being? When are we going to stop being just a "human doing" and start being a "human being?"

"Meditation keeps me grounded. It doesn't mean I am perfect. It means I have

A lot of people ask me what it is to sit with a master. Well, we were just having a small dialogue and to be honest he did not look very excited seeing me. It was kind of cute but maybe he was just mirroring me because in any case he said, "So you are leaving now?" and I said, "Yes," he said, "Where are you going" and I said, "I am going to California." And California was a magic word for Osho. Whenever I said I was going to California he all of a sudden got very excited about me. It's true! He said, "Many, many people come here after they have met you Krishna." But I had always been an asshole for Osho, I just loved it. I felt on fire, I felt in love and when I met people it was contagious. And I was an unusual guy. I would lead meditations, but everybody in the West was paying to meditate at that time, giving hundreds of dollars to Maharishi Mahesh Yogi to get a mantra that often times just put them even deeper asleep. But what I would do is, I would actually pay people if they would meditate. I would go to the Salvation Army and I would buy a hundred white T-shirts. I think they were around fifty cents at the time and then for another fifty cents I dyed them orange because that was the color we wore to have us feel like a family.

This was meditation together; a family that meditates together stays together. So I used to give everybody an orange T-shirt, then I would take them to the beach in Venice, California and I would instruct them to breathe for ten minutes and then I instruct them to let go for ten minutes, screaming, yelling. And the most beautiful thing about the ocean is that it could always accept madness. We never had problems with police, we never had problems with authority, and the ocean itself is such a wild experience that when twenty or so fools are screaming at the top of their lungs, it's almost like being thrown into a giant washing machine. Many times we ended up swimming at the end of the meditation, we

the guts to look at my life and enjoy it more." Batul

were so relaxed. Anyway Osho was very, very interested that I was going to California and he asked, "What are you going to do there?" Well, at that time as I was with a fabulous girl called Krishna Priya, very sensitive, totally different than me. I said to Osho, "I am gonna go to California and Krishna Priya just got a degree in teaching autistic children, so we have a concept where we're gonna get a country place and live with autistic children and each of these children would have their own teacher and each of these teachers, as far as we were concerned, will be a sannyasin because we know how to be with autistic kids. It's gonna be a wonderful total experience." I would run the place and Krishna Priya, who was a delight and had had a lot of success in this field, was offered this chance to start a school for autistic children where it was just too difficult for them to live at home. And Osho said to me, "Well, I tell you what Krishna Prem, you go to America first, you go directly to California and you find a place that would be appropriate for a school and when you do I will send Krishna Priya back. Right now she needs to be here longer." I did not quite understand it and in fact I never saw Krishna Priya again as my girlfriend but that's another story.

There I am in California looking for a property for the school and the funny thing about it is Osho said to me in darshan right before I left, "Make sure you get a vehicle big enough for the two of us." I did not understand what he meant but what I did was I went out taking all my remaining money and bought a car because for me a vehicle and a car were the same thing at that time. So I was sitting there in my car because I had put all my money into this car and therefore did not have any insurance and I did not even have any gas. I was on unemployment benefit at the time so I did not have much money, but I did have the car and so I basically lived in it. And I went to do this Dynamic meditation that was

"Many a man has fallen in love with a girl in a light so dim he would not have

being held at a yoga center in San Diego, and I did that Dynamic because I was brought up to have insurance and I was also brought up to have gas money, and there I am with a car and nothing else and I let it rip in that meditation, I really had a good scream. In those days I just screamed a lot. I did that meditation quite a bit, Dynamic meditation. At the end of the meditation I met a guy named Ron Modec. He was a real-estate agent and we just liked each other. I came into the meditation still in my orange robe and in my long beard and he came to the meditation in a suit and tie. I liked that.

So after the meditation he tightened up his tie and I freshened up my robe and we went out for a cup of coffee, and we had a great time. We got very, very excited talking to each other and he asked me what I want to do in my life. Basically I said, "Well, what I would really like to do is start a Greek gymnasium. What I mean by that is that people would throw themselves into the body either through Dynamic meditation or playing tennis or lifting weights or dancing or making love, but at the end of the meditation or at the end of the activity I should say instead of the usual bla bla bla, you know gossip, gossip, gossip; "Now that we play tennis together, will you sleep with me?" "Now that we danced together will you marry me forever?" No, instead of the bla bla bla at the end of activity we would all lie down and relax for fifteen minutes to renew ourselves. We would spend all our energy in activity, lie down on the ground together to relax and have the energy return. That was my concept of a Greek gymnasium, I don't know if it's even true but I love the concept. We got really excited and it was amazing when the bill came for the two cups of coffee, it turned out that I did not have any money and neither did he. And we laughed and I looked at the waitress and she looked at me and I am a little embarrassed to say this but I gave her a one dollar food

chosen a suit by it." Maurice Chevalier

stamp and she just smiled and we left. And then it turns out that Ron really liked this concept and said, "You know, I sell real-estate out in Lucerne Valley, just outside Apple Valley, California and I get paid fifty dollars to show property." So we called his sister and borrowed ten dollars and we put ten dollars in the gas tank and we drove to Lucerne Valley to look at property in the high desert. It was two, two and a half hours east of Los Angeles and it was very exciting. And I saw the possibility that I could do something here; I couldn't afford LA, I couldn't even really afford to sleep in my car in LA because the parking charges were too expensive, but anyway, here I am and as Ron showed me the property, his boss slipped him fifty dollars and asked him who this weirdo was, but I am acting very interested and I look at the owner and the owner looks at me. I said to them, "I am gonna buy this place." Then Ron called me aside and he said, "Look, I have already got the fifty dollars, let's give my sister back her ten dollars and let's leave." And I said, "Ron, I am gonna buy this place and I am gonna buy it right away and I am gonna start an ashram for Osho based on what we talked about." He said, "Really? You don't have any penny, how are you gonna do this?" And I said, "Well, would you like to be involved?" He said, "I would love to be involved, how can I be involved?" And I said, "Well, I am going to take your commission if I buy this place and give it as a donation so that we can get started." He said, "You are so crazy, I will do it because you don't have a chance to buy this place, I just wanna leave." I said to the owner, "I will be back," and the owner said, "You know, I think you will be."

And what happened that night is I just got on the phone because I needed 30,000 dollars right away for the down payment. My god, I called all those people that I gave orange T-shirts to and I said, "I found a place where we can live together and meditate together

"Let the lover be disgraceful, crazy, absent-minded. Someone sober will worry

and then advertise that people could come from LA and spend the weekend there." I got 15,000 dollars in my pocket within a few days, but I needed 30,000 dollars in my pocket. So I have a very wealthy brother, every meditator that has nothing has a wealthy brother. I don't know but this may be a Jewish phenomenon. They say in the Jewish world that either my son is a millionaire or my son is a priest or a rabbi. But there I was with my older brother and I said to my older brother, "I have got 15,000 dollars and I need 30,000 dollars. 15,000 don't do me no good at all, so I will tell you what we are gonna do. I am gonna put 15,000 dollars on the table and you are gonna write out a check for 30,000 dollars and we are gonna flip the coin. If you win you keep my money, if I win I take the check." I was shitting my pants, my brother looked like he was shitting his pants too, but somehow he is cooler about money than I am and he had to add to the equation that I was just hungry, I wanted this so very, very much. We flipped the coin and I won, he took the 15,000 in cash, I took the 30,000 dollar check and I went back to the property and I put that check on the table. I said to the owner, "You're gonna have to hold the paper, but here is the 30,000 dollar down payment." He said, "I will hold the paper because I wanna get out of here just as much as you wanna get in here." And we struck a deal that made my real-estate agent friend shit in his pants because he has just given up his commission to me. Anyway we put the money down; it's the fastest deal of all time!

What I'd bought was a dude ranch for girls who come up from the city and they ride their horses through the desert and they have a great time, and then they go home. The owner was a real cowboy. He was cleaning his rifle, counting his horses, looking at those girls and making sure everything is fine, thanking God that he was gonna get rid of this property and I was playing with my

69

about events going badly. Let the lover be." Rumi

beads and thanking Osho for getting this property. I was on fire and he was thrilled, there was no mistake about it. I don't know what to say. I mean, I am sitting in a robe with a beard but I felt like a cowboy. I felt like I could do anything. And we sent the check just down the road, a mile away to the Lucerne Valley National Bank, (it's probably a Bank of America by now,) and they rushed that check through because it's gold and the check bounced, "Insufficient funds!" "My god," I said to Ralf, the guy selling the property, "I need to make a collect call." So I made the collect call and I said to my brother, "Max, if you weren't my brother, I wouldn't even tell you that I am going to borrow this guy's rifle that he just cleaned, I wouldn't even tell you that I am gonna borrow his rifle and a bullet and come and kill you. I wouldn't even tell you. But since you are my brother I am warning you right now, I am on my way, I am coming to see you; you're a mother-fucker." And he chuckles over the phone and he said to me, "The check is not good. I do not gamble, I am loaning you 15,000 dollars, you are going to pay me back. But I know you come from the same genes that I have and I know that the only way this deal could work is if you were ready to kill for it and that's the risk I took with you. If you accept the responsibility of a 15,000 dollar debt, I am happy to call the bank now and tell them that the check is good." It was like Zen in America, I don't know how to explain it to you but my brother and I fell in love in that moment. I totally got what he was saying, life is not a gamble. Life is a calculated risk. You go for it, you are total and then it will work. If you sleep-walk or you think you just won 15,000 dollar in a crap-shoot, there is a better chance that it won't work. It may still work by the way but in this case I got it, my brother was teaching me a lesson which I had never allowed him to teach me before. And from that moment I was in business. And I tell you right now while that check was bouncing, all over the great LA area the dust was

"Those who were dancing were thought to be insane by those who could not

coming off the wheels of my friends' cars coming up the half-mile driveway to live with me. If that check wasn't good, actually I don't know if I would have made it to my brother to kill him. I probably would have been shot by these people; they had given me all their money to start a dream.

Anyway, turns out that check was good and Ralf was great, he immediately started packing up his rifles. I tell you the funniest thing that happened in that moment, up the driveway come fifteen hippies with beards. Meditators I would call them, I don't know if they were hippies because we were finished with drugs for the moment at least. And there we are and a number of cars coming up the driveway, just as Ralf's girl-scouts came riding down from the hills. At that same moment an Indian friend of Osho jumps out of the car, throws off his robe and starts screaming, "Osho, Osho, Osho." I couldn't believe it, it was a miracle because I could see myself getting in trouble right away. The good news is that Ron Modec was such a handsome man and such a good real-estate agent that he is standing there within three feet of this naked Indian who is screaming, "Osho, you have done it! This is it! This is it, nirvana!" All the girls could see was Ron Modec and it was a beautiful lesson again, because why would a fifteen year-old girl give a shit about a naked, hundred year-old Indian? All they could see was this gorgeous real-estate agent. Thank you so much, I was so happy about it. Anyway, here we are. The girls leave, the Indian guy gets dressed again and we all sit down for dinner. It was such a beautiful incident. We were home. And the place was ours. Ralf did not give a shit about the furniture, he left the horses, we did not want to keep horses but we kept a couple just for fun.

So Ralf took his 30,000 dollars and drove down the driveway and there we are. The funny thing is that when you meet me I will probably be looking pretty rich, but at that time I did not have a

71

penny to my name, nothing. And I guess I created that in the strangest ways, thirty years ago we are talking, just through being here and now. I never had a penny in my pocket at the end of each day, from the time I was ten till the time I was forty. I was rich in the morning and broke in the evening. I never missed a meal and I never had money for breakfast. I don't know how to explain this, I had a lot of guts, I had a lot of fun, and I did not want to accumulate wealth. In a sense I saw it as a difficulty. I don't know, I have to look into it more. All I can say is that being here and now and being broke had so much in common.

And here I was, now we'd got this place, there is no food in the fridge except what Ralf left and we were vegetarian at that time and god, he'd left only meat in the fridge. What to do with meat? We just brought it down to the local church and gave it away as a donation. And here we are with no money. The first thing that happen of course, is the gasman comes up. I did have, I think it was, a thirty-five dollar deposit for the gasman because I had been warned that he was coming up. So I had thirty-five bucks for the gasman. But we had two gas meters, which meant he wanted seventy dollars and I will never forget it, he was coming to the second meter, he did not know me. I swear to god, I am embarrassed to say this but I took off all my clothes and I am really a hairy person. I had hair on my head at that time, I had hair on my face at that time, I was covered with hair. I actually looked like I had clothes on, that's how much hair I had. I had so much hair people called me Hairy Krishna. And the gasman looks at me and it was really funny. I said to him, "They took my clothes. They took my clothes." I acted like I was totally crazy but delightful. And he just turned around and got on his truck with the same thirty-five dollars check that I had given to him while I was dressed on the other side of the property, he just did not recognize

"Love can only be real if it begins with yourself. Without love inside how can

me and why does he want a problem like that? So he drove away and then we were sitting there at night not eating, some people of course had food in their trucks and in their pick-ups and in their cars and there was about twenty of us by now, so we managed to eat. And we had a meeting and I said, "My god, we have the place but we don't have anything else." And it is amazing people just shared whatever they had, but we weren't into taking donations so we wrote down what everybody had and they were credited with living there and that's how we did it. That's how we started and we never looked back.

I knew right from the beginning that I would never see Krishna Priya again as my girlfriend. I knew right from the beginning of Geetam, which is the name Osho gave to this place, which means the song of Krishna; I knew what he meant now. I got us a vehicle big enough for all of us and I also knew that I was gonna be working with mentally disturbed people for the rest of my life, but they weren't going to be autistic children, they were going to be people just like you and me.

Geetam was on seventy acres which is a pretty big piece of property. It had eleven small buildings and one building big enough to house meditations, and the other ten were where we could sleep and have an office. We were successful right away just because there were fifteen of us and we all had fifteen friends and it was a unique experience. It did not have qualities of a luxurious California spa, it was just a rough and ready place to let go and to be and that's exactly what I wanted to buy. But I will never forget it was also a place where we began to take things off and the first thing we did was take our clothes off. We tried to keep it to just at the pool and at the volleyball court, but sooner or later we were just naked. I mean, we were in the desert and we were naked. And the good thing about naked is the only people that would visit us

73

were people that were willing to be naked. So even though we were in the red-neck part of California, the last thing you want to see at that time was a bunch of naked people. Not even the police would come for the first two months. And then one day the sirens of the local police came roaring up the driveway. We did not even have time to put our clothes on and I well remember that I was naked in the office and my secretary, Gangotri, was also naked. She had her legs up almost like she was at the gynecologist's, and the cops just came in and they couldn't believe it. I know it sounds wild, I hope you can put this in perspective of thirty-plus years ago in California, but it wasn't an unnatural thing to be naked. If the weather was perfect we were naked. And the cops were really funny, they couldn't look at Gangotri for sure. The younger cop said that there had just been a robbery at the local gas station and we have reason to believe that the gentleman concerned came to your property. And Gangotri said, "Well what does he look like?" The guy said, "Well, the fugitive had on blue jeans and he had a blue jeans shirt, a cowboy hat and cowboy boots." And Gangotri said, "Get real, what does he look like naked?"

And we just started laughing including the cops; it was very, very funny and then we brought a couple of what we call lungis, it's basically a piece of material from India that you wrap around your waist so it looks like a long, straight skirt, and Gangotri wrapped herself up and I wrapped myself up and that kind of broke the ice. The cop then said, "There really hasn't been a robbery, we have just been unable to think of a reason to come to visit you folks, you don't do anything wrong but you also don't do anything right." So we laughed again and what really broke the ice is that the older cop was gonna get married and he was gonna marry a yoga teacher and she wanted to visit our property and that's when we started to put clothes back on because basically what he said is,

74

"Dance so totally that the dancer is no longer there, but only the dance

"I would like to bring her up to visit you and I can understand that you might be naked at the pool area but I don't think that I wanna bring my fiancé to your property if you are gonna be naked all over the place. So if we have lunch with you like you are suggesting, you have to wear clothes because I can't go back down town and say you guys were naked when we had our lunch. It's just not appropriate and I strongly suggest that you listen to me." And it was really cute and we had a big meeting and we were actually getting very popular by now. We decided at that point to have nudity only at the pool and of course the volleyball court, which was right by the pool and still I can remember many experiences playing naked volleyball. I am not much of a swimmer but I am a pretty good volleyball player. But anyway, that was a small area and it was a space you did not have to visit if you didn't want to, because it was only a quarter of an acre on this seventy-acre piece of property. So that was the naked area from then on. I loved the cops for helping us to see that for what it was, and of course he brought his girlfriend up and she was ecstatic with the openness and the wildness and the fact that we did yoga to be ready to meditate instead of to do yoga to be ready to do yoga.

We got more and more popular when we put our clothes back on. But it was cool; you could wear a bathing suit or you did not have to wear a bathing suit. And for volleyball of course you could wear clothes; it was not easy to play naked volleyball. Most people wore at least a sports bra, and there are always some people that are going to insist that that was the naked area. And I never forget that there was a girl there named Maniko. She had a small son named Forest and she was breast-feeding him. She was pulling up her blouse and her sweater and Forest was against her breast and you could just see a very small sliver of skin of Maniko's breast. I am now in India and I am sitting with Osho's secretary, Laxmi,

remains." Osho

and she shows me this picture of Maniko breast-feeding her son. She looks at the picture, I look at the picture, she said, "Do you see anything unusual about this picture?" And I said, "No, I don't. In America many woman breast-feed their children in public." And she said, "Well, in India we breast-feed children in public but there is something that is very disturbing." And I looked at the picture and I could not figure out what could possibly be disturbing. Laxmi looked at me and said, "I can see part of Maniko's breast." Now I am talking about a smallest sliver of skin, I don't even know if it's breast, it could have been her shoulder, where the shoulder meets the breast, I don't know what they call that area. Anyway I couldn't believe it and Laxmi said, "Geetam is getting very popular now and we cannot afford a situation where people are naked." And I was laughing on the inside and I am sure that Laxmi was also laughing at me on the inside because now Geetam was world-famous for being absolutely natural, absolutely wild, absolutely Osho, and we had no rules except to treat each other well and I heard it right away. It was like another Zen lesson, there is no need for Laxmi to talk about the past, there is no need to bring up nudity, no need to bring up the wildness, she looked at me and she said, "No more nudity at Geetam."

So then the rules changed. From then on everybody had to bring a lungi to the volleyball court, and to the swimming pool area, and there they could either wear a bathing suit or not wear a bathing suit. But as soon as they left that area, they had to put their lungi or some kind of clothing on. And we never heard from Poona again. I never heard from Laxmi again. Somewhere I think she would love to have said, "You have to wear clothes even in the swimming-pool." I don't know if you have ever been to India, but Indians are always dressed when they go in the water. Very dressed, from head to toe they wear their clothes when they are in the water. At least,

76

"Neither birth nor death are in our hands. Once you realize this, prayer arises.

they did when I was first there. All the Indian boys have their white underwear, you know, the kind that says Calvin Klein but is a knock-off. Indians generally don't wear Calvin Klein unless it is a knock-off. If Calvin Klein ever wants to make money, he can go to the beach and ask everybody to pay him a dollar, because you know they did not pay to wear his name, they have got it for free.

Calvin Klein is everywhere. In fact, I think you might have heard that famous story when Calvin Klein's daughter said, "I never get laid. I never get laid." And when the announcer asked why she did not get laid, she answered, "I always see my father's name right before the boy gets naked. And I cannot make love – my father is in the room." I don't know if that is a true story or not, but I like it.

I began to wear clothes also. It felt good. I like clothes.

One of the wild things that happened one time was my brother of course felt really good about the support that he had given me and he felt great that he was paid back. And he and his wife actually came to visit and they wouldn't stay over, they stayed in a hotel and when they did come to visit they were treated like honored guests. They came to dinner and we were still naked at the time. I wore a small lungi out of respect but everybody else was naked except for me in my small lungi and my brother and sister-in-law. And they loved the place. They did not agree with anything of course; they did not agree with Osho and they did not agree with the nudity but they could understand the life energy. People were laughing, people were giggling, people were generous, people were genuinely glad that they were there. It had that vibe of love that you get when people love together and meditate together. They respect each other. And my brother and his wife were feeling it. Anyway they had said they would go after Sunday lunch, and

77

my sister-in-law got up to leave and this guy named Dinesh got up too quickly and his penis was basically big, huge. I was very jealous and he stood up and I swear to god, his machinery was in her face and she was great. She made like its normal, she stood up, shook his hand and just left. And I don't think he remembers the incident but every time I see her she still remembers, she still brings it up. And I think that's kind of cute, he doesn't remember but she remembers. That was a moment in her life.

Other stories about Geetam include when we eventually sold the place for half a million dollars. My family was really excited that I turned 15,000 dollars into a 30,000 dollar down payment. I paid the other 15,000 back to my brother, no interest of course, and my brother called me and congratulated me, "450,000 of 500,000 dollars! You are rich, congratulations, you are a Mogul." And I said, "Max, are you sitting down?" he said, "Yes" and I said, "Max, I just donated the whole 500,000 dollars to Osho, he is coming to America." My brother nearly shit his pants but somewhere I could almost hear him say, "I Zen that guy out five years ago with a flip of a coin and now he has done it back to me. As much as I got him to hold on, that is as much as this boy is letting go." I think somewhere there was a respect for what I did, but also he couldn't believe it. It's not in his nature and I have learned to love him for his nature, he has learned to kind of like me for my nature and that's the name of the game.

Osho preferred the word currency to money. Currency suggests a flow, easy come, easy go. I agree with the easy go part. I am more like a yogi than a master when it comes to the green stuff.

A yogi in New York City stops at a hot dog stand and orders his lunch: "Make me one with everything."
The yogi gives the vendor a $20 bill.

78

"Don't keep yourself separate. Don't remain aloof, cold. Don't remain just a

The vendor takes the $20 and gives the yogi his hot dog.

The yogi waits a beat. The vendor just smiles at him.

"Surely this hot dog didn't cost twenty bucks! Where's my change?"

And the vendor replies, "Ah, but change must come from within!"

And one more funny that is right on the money;

Krishna Prem: "Osho?"

Osho: "Yes?"

KP: "Can I ask you something?"

Osho: "Of course!"

KP: "What is a million years for you?"

Osho: "A second."

KP: "And a million dollars?"

Osho: "A penny."

KP: "Osho, Can you give me a penny?"

Osho: "Wait a second."

Geetam was becoming a bigger and bigger ashram in America, for Osho and people were coming left, right and center to get a taste of Osho's dynamic meditations. And more often than not it was a fast track to booking a ticket to ride. My instructions were always clear: enjoy being here as it was a springboard to meditation, and to getting up the guts to make the jump to Pune. At the same time in Pune, Osho was sending people into therapy as a means to an end. Therapy cleans your basement and meditation cleans your attic but my concern was that the therapy groups were rumored to be full of sex and violence and getting wilder by the moment. I could feel my ass tighten every time I suggested a friend take the jump. Not only was I Osho's man in America, I also became a travel agent in order to offer inexpensive flights and

79

spectator, become a participant." Osho

make money for the ashram in America as well. Above and beyond the money I made as a travel agent, I would also go to LAX to wish a bon voyage. At that time if any flight had fifteen people on it, the airlines gave us one ticket for free. Picture this: I'm at the airport, I count the number of heads and there's fifteen friends going to see Osho, so I became the free ticket! Armed with only a passport and my personality, I boarded the plane.

Sitting in front of Osho, I said to him, "It's easy for me to tell people to come and see you but I hope you're not going to suggest I do any of these funny groups you're recommending. Even though I'm beyond therapy, your guidance scares the shit out of me!" Without missing a beat Osho said, "I suggest the Encounter group." I certainly was beyond shitting my pants, but in reality I was glad I was wearing underwear – the thought of doing it myself instead of suggesting someone else do it, I was humbled by fear, and fear makes time appear solid. When I entered the chambers the very next morning the therapist had a little smile on his face and the nineteen participants looked just like me. The good news, and I may be coming from hindsight at this point, was that this was the safest space I've ever been in which to have a fight. Many people came to Osho, and to meditation, because they were good people, loving people, avoiding sex and violence their whole lives because it felt ungodly and they'd been told that it was. Osho simply was not about avoidance, and he also wasn't in favor of a mix of sex and violence outside of this environment.

Right away this truth appeared in my face. A young man stood up and said, "I hate my father, I want to kill him!" The therapist asked him who in the room looks like his dad? Of course it was me. Without missing a beat this man regressed into a young boy, who pounced on this young man who felt like the boy's eighty year-old father. Just as he was about to kill me with a scissor-lock

80

on my neck, I recited the Lord's Prayer for the first time in my life. There was no question in my mind that I did not have a future and just as I was about to take my last breath the boy burst into tears, took his legs from around my neck, rolled into a fetus position, and cried until lunch time. It simply had nothing to do with me, and I'm glad to tell you that. Just before lunch the therapist told me that my beard, which I was very proud of, was not only growing long, but it was growing out and it was separating me from everyone in the group. I didn't have to ask; instead of having lunch I went to M. G. Road and had a shave. Ten years of red growth not only separated me from you, but it separated me from looking like my family. When I came back into the room the therapist had me look in the mirror and instead of seeing a male seeker of the truth, I saw my brother insisting I learn how to box so that the Nazis would not be able to take advantage of me if it ever happened again. Immediately the boxing gloves were brought out of the therapist's tool kit. The therapist put the gloves on me and said, "Who looks like your brother?" Lo and behold the same man that just about beat the shit out of me in the morning, had that glint in his eye that simply said "older brother." With glee the therapist tied the laces of my imminent demise. We were toe to toe and I beat the shit out of that guy before you could say knockout. As I stood over him I too burst into tears. That was the last fight I've been in. You probably know more about violence than I do, so I really can't be your teacher in this moment, I can only suggest that the outcome of violence is a peaceful, easy feeling. It thrills me to know that violence can end and that peace can begin. It takes more awareness to know when to put violence away and when to bring it up; and without awareness peace will turn to violence. It's not that violence ends and peace begins, it's that awareness appears and you lose your need to act. Often times, without awareness, a simple scratch on your conditioning, and there will never be peace in your

of being. You simply are." Osho

Sinai Desert, in your Vatican, or wherever you live that remains unconscious. Awareness is another word for no beginning, no end. Awareness is a white screen and your life is merely a projection.

Again you become the center and your life simply remains a cyclone. So let me ask you this question: are you a Jew or are you a Christian or are you awareness who's brought up as a Jew or a Christian? When are you going to finally realize that before you were conceived, your life was not defined by an organized religion, and when you die you won't get a bible when you enter the unknown?

For me the group was already over after just one day. Looking into violence was the risk that I felt I hadn't taken yet, since I was a young boy who presumably didn't know any better. The only thing I remember about fighting as a young man is the lie that I was told by every bully older than me, that the first person that throws a punch wins the fight. I want to dispel that rumor right now, and please don't make fun of my nose when you see me in person. My feeling was that for the next six days of the group I could watch everybody else travel through their shit while I relaxed on my throne. About the fourth day of the group, of witnessing other people fucking and fighting, the group leader looked at me and said, "Come up with something that you need to still work on, or get out of Dodge." My inner reaction to this outer statement was that the group leader could see something that I was avoiding. I asked myself what risk I never took on the sexual level. Having founded Geetam, and having lived there for years, I was the first man that every divorcee in Southern California met when they decided Osho was the answer to their frustration. The weekend groups at Geetam were also about sex and violence, but as I never thought of doing a group there because I was working, I was fully aware that on that Saturday night, second night of the

82

Encounter group, the group leader would announce that it was time to take a risk. So I would position myself with a cup of tea, half naked on the Zen bench in front of the group hall. Invariably I became a sex object; I can only describe this with the generalization that I died and went to heaven every Saturday night for years at a time, and even though I was an ugly fucker the women were blinded by their homework assignment. Having said that, I was never invited to meet anybody's parents; with the beard down to my toes and not a penny in my pocket, I simply was not marriage material. I had to live with this and keep moving from one Saturday night to the next Saturday night. I know you probably find this hard to believe, and so do I. It was a sad day when Geetam was sold and I became an alcoholic trying to remember every Saturday night of the past five years. By now it may be true, it may never have happened.

Suddenly fear gripped me as I realized the only risk I have never taken sexually was to be with a man. The kinkiest thing I'd ever done was I had a pair of high heels at work and when I wrote the girls' questions for the Dating Game television show, I went off and slipped into my stilettos to sharpen my female intuition. I have nice calf muscles. Other than that I can remember as a very young man, before my teens, I could feel the sexual advances of certain older boys and instead of teaching me about sexuality, they taught me about power. I simply was never that interested in homosexual activity. Of course having spent years in Hollywood as a writer I met many other young, creative men whose inclination was gay. As gay as my friends were, that's how straight I felt. It's pretty simple to me: I just like women. Nature agreed with me, my conditioning agreed with me, my eyes were always attracted to tits and ass, my world was straight-ahead heterosexual. As far as I was concerned, if every man in the world were gay, I would die in

83

heaven from a heart attack, satisfying the other fifty percent of the world. Praise the Lord! If I ever had a question, it was not about me, but how was it possible to be gay? As this group was about experience beyond thought, I simply went down on the guy sitting in a full lotus beside me. I think he was as surprised as I was. How did this change my life? I learned then and there that I had no electricity being with a man. But I did find myself in an uncompromising position, the question in my mind was, how the fuck do I get out of this situation before this guy comes all over my face? Even today I'm embarrassed that you have to read this, but I am assuming that you have made the same mistake once. Funnily enough I had my eyes closed, which caused a small smile in me as I always close my eyes when I'm making love. My inner giggle brought a tear to my eye, and when I took a moment off the job in hand, I observed that I was surrounded, not by six other gay men, but by a half a dozen gorgeous women whose question was, "I've always wanted to know how to give great head?" And who better to ask than the biggest gay in the world, me! I had so much fun over the next three days teaching women how gay men give fellatio. They remain grateful that I was able to experience and teach at the same time. So at this time I'd like to apologize to those six women because each one felt that she was the one that turned me straight.

And before you jump on a plane to Pune, to learn to fuck and fight, Osho's instructions were that this part of the work was complete unto itself. That he wanted all of his sannyasins to learn from their mistakes, and there are subtle ways to becoming a loving, peaceful human being without acting out in an immature way. As much as I know now about love, I'm sure glad I had a chance to be in that room for one week acting out in a safe space.

"Abundance is the very nature of existence; that richness is the very core; that

To this day I would not consider fighting or fucking with someone I didn't love.

When Osho was arrested in America he was in the company of several police officers, and one of the young men in question had a soft spot for Osho. At one point Osho screamed at him and asked that officer to treat him like a human being. When the young man was alone with Osho he had the courage to ask, "I'm the one that loves you, why did you scream at me?" And Osho simply said, "It would do me no good to scream at someone that hates me, and if it woke you up then it was a great scream."

Each day for the last four mornings of the group I had a blow-job for breakfast along with my orange juice. I saved the most beautiful girl for last, and long after my last sip of orange juice the girl came up for air and said, "You must be gay." I simply had nothing left to come. And she said if I was ever serious about changing, to please call her right away. But I am not interested in wasting energy.

I smiled to myself and realized that monogamy was not all it was cracked up to be, and that I didn't want to create any offspring whenever I sprang a leak. I decided to have a vasectomy. At the time it was free in California but you had to convince a doctor that you were sure that you weren't making a mistake, because although the operation is reversible, it's difficult. Once he agreed with me that the world would be a better place without me in the future, he smiled and said, "Before you come in next Tuesday morning for your operation, it would be a natural anesthetic to have two orgasms." I knew exactly what he meant as I remembered that beautiful blonde bobbing up and down.

existence does not believe in poverty." Osho

At the end of every group Osho would call together all the participants for darshan. In that very darshan after the encounter group, Osho said that the new phase of his work was much more subtle, that the sword of awareness makes enlightenment possible without fighting with your best friends, and without making love. And Osho spoke of Atisha's heart meditation, breathing in and breathing out, again the word "and" is so very important, it's not about breathing in or breathing out, life is really a circle of breath. Even today I practice this meditation, and even though I believe Osho, oftentimes I must admit that I want to kill someone when they don't agree with me, and making love to a total stranger is the only thing that helps to relax me. All joking aside, I want you to consider Atisha and his meditation every day for three months. The world has to change, and change begins with you. For once I'm being very serious. In every single one of us there's not only a St Francis of Assisi, there's also a Hitler. It was fine for me to think of myself as St Francis, but difficult for me to look at the Hitler inside. Osho told us that awareness will set you free, and that the good and the bad in everyone again is just an experience and is not who you are.

I did what any horny, single man would do in such a dire situation; I put up a "can you help me" sign in the dishwashing area of the kitchen at Geetam. For two days no one signed up – I was mortified. Most of my lovers came up the driveway for just a weekend but I was sure someone on the staff would come to my aid in this, my hour of need. When a young girl named Yoganidra decided to leave the ashram in haste in search of living alone, I snuck into the kitchen pretending to wash dishes and scribbled her name beside the number one spot out of four places, and somehow that did the trick. Just before the appointed hour Leela signed on the dotted line and I was pretty excited 'cause I fancied Leela quite

"Remember one thing: that you should not leave this earth unless you have

a bit. As any brilliant meditator would do, I decided to masturbate first and see Leela second. I closed my eyes and I imagined that beauty that never got me off in Pune, accomplishing the mission in hand while a glass of orange juice was left unattended. Leela knocked on the door and we shared a glass of orange juice and got down to business. The doctor asked me if I had done my homework, and when I couldn't wipe the smile off my face he simply said, "Let's get started."

So the first time I came to India I was in Goa and I was living under a cashew tree with my girlfriend Krishna Priya. We were really living au naturel and the weather was just perfect and the sky was full of stars, the sea was crashing at our knees, it was really, really natural and beautiful. Krishna Priya and I were having an ideal time just being in love under the stars. But I don't know if you ever have been to India, maybe you have been to Mexico, maybe you remember Montezuma's Revenge? India has a very similar experience, Delhi Belly, and for lack of a better upbringing, I call it the shits. It comes from doing ordinary things like drinking a glass of water, and my god, life just becomes a toilet. I don't know what to say, you just shit your pains out, you shit your emotions out, you become, for lack of a better word, shitty. And I think that one of the reasons relationships go to pot, at least in the East, is very simple. You drink the water and your life gets shitty. Anyway Krishna Priya and I hadn't any awareness, we didn't know how to deal with this very much, we said we did not wanna talk to each other about this situation and one of the ways we dealt with this was to go to a local library and get books to read.

She got this absolutely enormous book called Autobiography of a Yogi by Yogananda. As I remember it, it had going on 1000 pages. I preferred smaller books, and I got a book called Seeds of Revolutionary Thought by Acharaya Rajneesh. Now when I say

87

this word Acharaya to you, I think you may get the same basic idea, what the hell is this word Acharaya? And when I don't understand a word I just skip over it. In fact in this situation I did not have any relationship with the word or the man Rajneesh at that very moment. So I absolutely did not bother reading his name. I just picked up this little book, which was about a hundred pages long. That was the book I got and that was the book that changed my life. So basically without saying anything Krishna Priya turned over onto her side of the coconut mattress under the cashew tree and I walked down the beach to watch the sunset. I began to read this book and it was really good. I loved it, I loved it and I loved it. Basically it was just what the doctor ordered and I really liked it. I had put my lungi down and put my shoes between page two and three so I would not lose my place, went up to the chai shop and I got myself a pot of herb tea. Certainly I could not drink coffee because I was already shitting and certainly I couldn't take anything with caffeine at that moment and certainly I did not have any drugs anywhere near me. I say this because sometimes when I feel good, at that point of my life I might think about feeling even better. But when you are feeling lousy you just wanna clean up your act. Anyway, I can't really remember that far back. I know right now I am pretty much drug free but I am just accentuating this remark because I did not want anything in my body that would make me sick, therefore I was totally straight and I went back to the sea, back to my book, my lungi, that little piece of material you wear around you and then you lay it down so the sand does not go up the crack of your ass or wherever.

Conversely, now I am in India. And the California ashram is very, very successful. Every day in every way it is happening, it is growing. We are alive. Absolutely. And it is a magnet to people who do want to learn about meditation, who are not afraid of also

"You have to remember that freedom is the highest value, and if love is not

being alive. Most people learn to meditate so that they can sedate themselves naturally. Some people learn to meditate because they are alive and they just want to be alive even more.

Krishna Prem and I often wondered why Osho gave us the same name, because we thought we had so little in common, and he said that he felt that I was ecstatic about life and foolish about love and just the opposite was true for him. Both of us shared the feeling that having met Osho was such a highlight in our lives and fourteen years later we both felt dry as a bone in that moment, so we created a question together to ask Osho what he felt about this. Meeting him was such an explosion because we were innocent; we didn't come with the mind of an old meditator.

So here's our question;

BELOVED MASTER,

WHEN I FIRST SAT IN FRONT OF YOU AT WOODLANDS, FOURTEEN YEARS AGO, THERE WAS AN EXPLOSION INSIDE. I DON'T KNOW WHAT IT MEANS, BUT I'VE OFTEN HAD THE FEELING THAT ALL I'VE BEEN TRYING TO DO EVER SINCE IS CATCH UP TO SOMETHING THAT HAS ALREADY HAPPENED.

Krishna Prem, the question you have asked has tremendous implications for all the seekers of truth, because it is a question which touches the very fundamental law of those who are in search of something inexplicable, something inexpressible.

Let me first make the law clear to you. It may have happened to many; it is going to happen to everybody. But you may not have taken the whole, comprehensive view. The law is that when you first meet the master you come innocent, without any experience.

89

You simply come as a receptivity, a sensitivity – ready to move into any dimension, willingly and totally. Hence, the first meeting with the master always brings an explosion.

The explosion happens because of your innocence, because of your unexpecting mind. You know nothing about spirituality, you know nothing about ecstasy. Your not-knowing is the cause of the explosion. But then begins a very troublesome journey. Then begins a nightmare. Then each and every moment you are waiting for that explosion to happen again. And you may wait for years – it will not happen, because you are not fulfilling the basic condition for its happening. You have forgotten completely in what situation the first explosion has happened.

Now there is no way to be again in that situation. Whatever you do there will be the expectation, the experience. You cannot create that not-knowing; that is not within your hands, and that is not the way existence functions. So the first thing you have to do, Krishna Prem, is to forget all about that explosion. It was good that it happened, but there are far greater things. Why bother about something so primary, a kindergarten experience....

(AN EXPLOSION – MORE LIKE A "POP" REALLY – HAPPENS WITH IMPECCABLE TIMING, AS FIRECRACKERS ARE SET OFF AT A NEIGHBORHOOD WEDDING CELEBRATION.)

You see? Just like that!

Start waiting for something greater. Of course you don't know what that

"Orgasm brings you naturally into a state of meditation: thinking disappears,

something will be.... (ANOTHER EXPLOSION! AND THE ASSEMBLY COLLAPSES WITH LAUGHTER. THE MASTER LOOKS AROUND, TENTATIVELY AND GRINNING.)

I am afraid that the moment I say anything more, it will happen again!

(A PAUSE TO LET THE HILARITY SETTLE.)

You start fresh.

You sit by my side, not expecting but waiting.

And try to understand the difference between expecting and just waiting. In expectation there is a desire and there is a clear-cut object that you are desiring. And that is blocking your progress. When you are just waiting, you don't know for what, the experience of just waiting is so precious, so valuable, so deeply transforming that something greater than the first explosion is bound to happen.

It will not be the same explosion. In these fourteen years so much water has gone down the Ganges. Neither you are you, nor am I the same person. Nothing is the same. The whole situation is changing every moment. And you get stuck with some beautiful moment and go on missing greater beauties and greater ecstasies.

Unhinge yourself.

Unless you drop that explosion and the expectation for it, you will remain fourteen years back, and between me and you there will be the gap of fourteen years. Just understand that it happened because you were not expecting it, and now it is not happening because you are expecting it.

91

the ego is no more. You are pure energy." Osho

Step 3: Resolve Your Challenge

Finally, as you experience and engage positively with all your pain and negativity – as you embrace all the thoughts, feelings, and self-criticisms that are driving your challenge – you find yourself spontaneously developing a new and more loving relationship with yourself. This new perspective on yourself naturally quiets the many strident voices of your challenge clashing in your mind, and almost immediately you begin to hear your true, authentic voice, your deep intuition, your TruSage. This voice is the real source of your healing power – it's where all your own best answers come from. And once you're able to listen to your voice, you quickly and effortlessly imagine creative ways to resolving your challenge. It's as if new ideas for health and happiness simply bubble up from your unconscious. And the more you listen, the more the craving, the pain, the fear – whatever your challenge – just dissolves away. It's really quite a miracle. And I don't use the world "miracle" very often.

That's all there is to it: 1-2-3. In no time at all, you'll be moving quickly through the process, feeling confident that you can manage your challenge, instead of having it manage you.

The above is an excerpt from the book The Voice: Overcome Negative Self-Talk and Discover Your Inner Wisdom by Dr. Brian Alman and Stephen Montgomery.

"Enlightenment is a meeting between an individual and the infinite whole." Osho

Chapter 4

Creativity: Unleashing the Forces Within

"To live in relationship and yet remain independent, that is what courage is. The new man will be courageous. In the past, only two kinds of cowards have existed on the earth, the worldly kind and the otherworldly kind – but both are cowards. The really brave man will live in the world and yet be not of it. Either this is going to happen, or a total destruction. Now there is no third alternative. Man cannot survive as he is. Either he has to change himself, transmute himself, or he has to die and vacate the earth."

The Book of Wisdom, Osho

Many athletes talk about getting in the zone. What they're referring to is doing an activity until they realize that they are no longer doing it, and it is happening by itself. Many marathon runners have reported that somehow after running and running for miles, they then get into a zone where they almost literally just sit back, relax and watch the running happening. It happened to me one time, after running eight miles. All of a sudden, I found my body was running while mysteriously I, or some part of me, was sitting back on my own shoulder, simply watching it all happen. Great; effortless effort!

Meditators experience the same thing; they get into a space where they start to see themselves doing things, yet feel they are not doing it. They are even watching themselves meditating. So, if we are somehow able to sit back and watch what the body is doing, then who are we and who is doing the doing? In spiritual circles,

"Set your life on fire. Seek those who fan your flames." Rumi people boldly say, "You are not the doer," but if you are not the doer, then who is? If you are not making it happen, then who is?

It's a very tricky question to answer, but for now let's just quote Frank Sinatra and say, "Do be do be do be dooo." It's not about doing OR being, it's about doing AND being both at the same time. In the small picture, our little local life, we're doing, while in the big picture we're just being. Life is not only about enjoying what you do; it's about enjoying who you're being too. Period.

Another interesting idea we have is that our things, our possessions or assets, somehow reflect who we are. In short, we are what we own. What we have helps either improve or discredit our image. So in order to be someone important, impressive and special, we not only need lots of things but preferably expensive ones. You guys will probably need a healthy bank account, a property portfolio and either a Mercedes or a Porsche, while you gals will probably need a gigantic diamond ring, rooms full of designer clothes and a set of luggage from Louis Vuitton. Then you're all set to party, hit the town and strut your stuff. And I'm no different than you. I always thought I needed a flash car to impress the chicks, and I needed a flash car and a flash chick to impress the guys, although, god knows why I thought I needed to impress the guys.

So there you are guys; you jump into your first Ferrari, you pay cash, and you're sitting in the driver's seat revving the engine. All of the sudden, right then, right there in the showroom, you feel for just a moment that there is nothing else you could possibly want in the world. You close your eyes and you think, "I am home, I have finally made it, and everything is now perfect." Then you open your eyes as the salesmen taps on the glass, you open your window

"Why do we wait with the moment so near. Be your own light. Keep your heart

and when he says your check has cleared you drive your spanking new car out of the showroom. But then, only two seconds later, you see a gorgeous, young blonde walking down the street, and immediately you think to yourself, "Now, if that blonde would just jump into this car next to me right now, I would have everything I want."

And there it is – for one moment, you have everything you want, you are home, you have made it, you are it, and the next you don't. It's like having an orgasm; for one second you are completely satisfied, your mind is silent, your body is relieved of tension and you are just lying there perfectly content. Then, in the next moment you are wanting to have sex again. For one glorious moment, in between one desire being fulfilled and another desire being launched, there is no desire at all. Then almost immediately, the mind jumps in again and says "I could have more!" "I could be even greater!" "Life could be even better!"

And that's the way it goes. Nothing wrong with it, that's just what the mind does. It thinks there's more, it convinces you there's more, and that even though you're doing OK, you're still not really complete. It desires more and more. That's the way it chatters on, "As long as you have more things… as long as you do what I want, you're going to be a great success." So all day long we're trading in our Mercedes Benz for a Rolls Royce in our heads, and believing we are that Mercedes Benz or that Rolls Royce. We spend our whole lives striving for bigger or better or faster things, constantly trying to upgrade who we are, when in reality we are just chasing our own tail.

But hang on a minute, are you what you have or own? Are you your California "got-it-all" mansion or your one-bed condo in Nowhereville? Are you your skateboard or your Lamborghini? Are

97

strong and sing your own song." Miten and Deva Premal

you your Wal-Mart discount card or your platinum American Express? Is this what you add up to? Now I'm not saying don't have a nice life, throw away all your nice things, renounce the world and pick up your begging bowl. No, enjoy them, in fact buy more, but just don't get caught up in thinking they're U or you need them to really be someone. Waking up to the true U, doesn't mean you shouldn't have that Ferrari, it means you know it's just a car.

Ah, now we get to the body. Let's face it; we're probably all pretty identified with our body. It's tricky not to think of ourselves as this huge lump of flesh and bone we carry around. I mean, who doesn't think of themselves in terms of their height or weight? Who doesn't notice if they are a small, medium, large or extra large? Who doesn't compare the color of their skin, hair and eyes, the size of their nose, ears and lips? What guy doesn't want huge pecs and a matching dick, what girl doesn't want slinky curves, pouty lips and perky tits? All the glossy magazines endorse the idea that we are our body, our style and our self-image. So we rush out and buy all the latest fashions, hair gels and lipsticks and pretty ourselves up, because we think that's who we are. We're the tag on our jeans and the name on our watch. We're our silicone cleavage, our collagen lips and our bleached smile. Cosmopolitan says so! But just because everyone else thinks something is true, doesn't mean it's necessarily so.

On a small iceberg, somewhere near the North Pole, a little bear goes up to his mother and asks, "Mom, what kind of bear am I?"

"You're a polar bear, son," replies his mother.

"Are you sure I'm not a brown bear?" he asks.

"Quite sure, son," she replies, "You're a polar bear."

98

"Accept yourself deeply with all your insecurities and fears. Stop believing that

But the little bear is not satisfied, "Mom," he says, "Maybe I'm a grizzly bear?"

The mother then asks him, "Why are you asking these questions, son? You're a polar bear."

So the little bear goes over to his father.

"Pop," he says, "Am I a panda bear?"

"No, son," says the father, "You're a polar bear."

"Not a koala bear?" asks the baby bear.

"No, a polar bear," says his father, "But, why are you asking all these questions?"

"Well," replied the baby bear, "if I'm a polar bear, then why am I so fucking cold?"

Maybe the little bear isn't a polar bear and maybe he isn't the stupid one here? Only because he repeatedly keeps being told he is a polar bear, does he come to believe this is so. It's the same with us. Because everyone around us keeps telling us that we are this body, so over time, we begin to stop questioning if it's true and begin to start believing it is so. And on top of thinking we're our body's vital statistics and looks, we're also thinking we're our body's age; "How old are you?" we gaily ask each other. "Oh, I'm twenty" or "I'm thirty" or "I'm forty-something," comes the reply! It might be more accurate to ask, "How old is your body?" and to answer, "Oh, twenty-one again!"

Our identification with our body isn't just confined to how old it is and the way it looks. Oh no, the story doesn't end there,

you are deficient." Krishnananda and Amana

there's our gender also. I mean, we must be male or female, a man or a woman, a guy or a gal.

Why do men have hair on their chests? Well, they can't have everything!

Then on top of that is our sexual orientation. Are we straight, bi or gay? I feel another joke coming on…

An old cowboy went into a bar and ordered a drink. As he sat there sipping his whiskey, a young lady sat down next to him. She turned to the cowboy and asked him, "Are you a real cowboy?"

"Well," he replied, "I've spent my whole life on a ranch, herding horses, mending fences and branding cattle, so I guess I am."

"I'm a lesbian," the young lady replied, "I spend my whole day thinking about women. As soon as I get up in the morning, I think about women. All day I think about women. Whatever I do, I think about women. When I take a shower, when I watch TV… everything seems to make me think of women."

A little later, a couple of tourists came into the bar, sat down next to the old cowboy and asked him, "Are you a real cowboy?" to which he replied, "I always thought I was, but I just found out I'm a lesbian."

Of course, we could then wander into the realms of sexual activity, and contemplate whether we are a total slut, frigid as the North Pole, or somewhere between the two. Whether we are our lacy bras, our PVC pants or our leopard-skin g-strings? Or maybe… let's not go down that road.

But look again; are you your body gender and your sexual orientation? Are you a "total man" with not an ounce of estrogen in

100

"A man who has himself for a guru has a fool for a disciple." Viramo your body? Are you "all woman" with not a molecule of testosterone in your body? Are you absolutely straight? Are you absolutely gay? Are you absolutely sure? Where is the dividing line? No really – where do U begin and end with the borders of your skin?

Guru sounds very simple, sounds cute if you just look at the four letters, but it actually took me over sixty years to get to this very moment. For most of my life I simply lived in the future, it was always gonna get better tomorrow for me. I don't know, but it started even as a young man, I just went to school and I said, "This school, it sucks. I can hardly wait till I am a man." Then I graduated school and I said, "Wow, the real world is pretty tough." And I did the best I could, but I never really got as depressed as you might think because I always simply thought that life was gonna get better. Even when I met my teacher and friend in India, this guy we call Osho, I still looked up to him and now I can see that this looking up to him was really, "In the future I can sit beside you." So even with my own teacher, even though he was always saying, "Be here and now," that just wasn't possible for me. Sure it looks very simple to say G U R U, but if you really look inside yourself you may see the same dilemma I had, that I am writing this book so that I can be myself. In fact I know now that I am myself and as soon as I found out that I am myself I also found out that you are you. Sounds foolish, sounds silly, I may even be wrong. Why do I say I may even be wrong because is there really an "I" to be wrong? In other words, my feeling about this lifetime is that I think that I am my feelings, I think that I am my thoughts, I think therefore I am. It's not true. You exist whether you know it or not, thinking is not who you are, feelings are not who you are.

" Beware the barrenness of a busy life." Socrates

Some fool said, "I think therefore I am," and it sounds so good that the whole West is based on that thought some way or another, I think therefore I am. It's really I am and I have the ability to think. One of the things that I am trying to say here is that we tend to look at ourselves as if our personality is real, as if our conditioning is real, as if religion is real, as if our sex is real. In another words we think that what we have been taught about who we are is real, and what this book is really about is getting back to not knowing who you are, getting naked, taking the risk of saying, "Don't tell me who I am. In fact I want to drop all thoughts that I have ever been told, even thoughts that came from my mind before I was silent enough to watch where these thoughts are coming from." In other words, who are you before you got a name? If I say, "Who are you?" most people say, "My name is Joe," or "My name is James." Who gives a shit what your name is! That's not the original question, that's not your original face, and I know I said this already but I'm repeating it because I want to emphasize this truth. So when a master says, "Who are you?" and if you say your name is James or Joe, he just begins to laugh at how you have failed to make enquiries into your own life. He is asking you, "What did you look like before your parents made love? What will you look like after you no longer have a body? What do you look like right now?" In the East this is referred to as your original face.

So you have changed tasks and there is a moment I suggest between when you took your hat off as the vice president of a bank and then you put on another hat, that you are not a daddy of a three year-old, there is a moment when you are no one at all. When you had a chance not to brag, not to have an ego, to be brand new and refreshed so that you don't say to your son, "I don't wanna play, I am still the vice president of the bank," and you have a chance to say, "Aha, right now I am your daddy, I have just been refreshed

"To be in meditation is to be one. No confusion, no hesitation. A response,

by a moment off when I wasn't the vice president and now I have some energy to play, I can be here now, brand new with you." And every father that has taken that moment to be with a child knows how fresh and new that child is. And that's what you wanna bring to your child, not the Jewish father, not that you are forty-five years old, not that you're exhausted, but you wanna bring to that moment the feeling that you are brand new and ready for right now. I call this getting out of your own way. It's very, very simple. You have got to stop being the vice president, you have got to stop being daddy, and you need to breathe into every moment. This doesn't mean that you space out, that you leave your body. It means to be present, to be a presence.

Often times Lao Tzu reminded us of this in his book Tao Te Ching, "Intelligent people know others, enlightened people know themselves." Your personality, your job, these are not your reality. Look at your son, does he have a religion? Or did you tell him that he has a religion. He might not even know he is a little boy, he just knows that he is alive. You probably are saying to yourself you don't have time to meditate. That means there are only twenty-four hours in a day, I have already been the vice president all day long, now I am a father tonight, when am I going to have time to meditate? In the East we always suggest that there are way more than twenty-four hours a day, in fact there is a Sufi tradition that says there are forty-eight hours in every day. In another words, twenty-four hours you are inside yourself talking to yourself, relating to yourself, and there are twenty-four hours a day when you are relating to others at work, or with your son. You have twenty-four hours inside of yourself where you are having an internal dialogue with yourself, and twenty-four hours a day you are talking and relating to the outside world. So basically there are forty-eight hours in a day.

a natural attitude happens in every moment." Tishan

You are simply too busy to give up your precious time simply to relax and let go. At least that's what I hear all the time from my friends when I return to Los Angeles, the City of Angels, from India. It took me the longest time to understand how busy Angels are.

Certainly you need a fast car to get from here to here. And funnily enough, I agree with you. Twenty-four hours is simply not enough time to have a successful life. So I want to offer you an extra twenty-four hours a day for "free" if you agree to set aside just one hour for meditation. Deal?

This is what I mean; the usual twenty-four hours is the time you spend away from yourself. It is the time you give your outer life, your job, your society, and your children. Look closely now: You also spend twenty-four hours a day on your inner self, talking to yourself, taking care of yourself. No wonder you are tired, every day of your life is forty-eight hours of work!

That's where meditation comes in. When you learn to meditate – or let's simply say when you learn to relax – there is no such thing as time. You are just in the moment. When your outer life and your inner life are in harmony, time disappears.

Here's a "lifework" assignment; to address that inner-outer harmony. Pick a juicy hour of your busy day and remain alert for one hour. Simply watch your two voices – inner and outer. A perfect example is being at dinner with a beloved. Watch your body eating and watch what comes out of your mouth at the same time. Witness what your mind is constantly repeating, "Is this food too fattening?" "I'd rather be alone." "Making love is less fattening."

"And this is the way of meditation: to find the extraordinary in the ordinary,

Remember the lifework assignment is to be alert, not to be honest. Relax. Be prepared. You just might rediscover that you are not the mind, not the body, that you are simply the witness. If so, give yourself an "A" for Enlightenment. If not, give yourself an "E" for Ego. In any case, have fun, it's your life.

And guess what? Now there is no such thing as time. Time analysis is created by conflict, what you are saying to yourself, and what you are saying to the other, were two opposite things and you just don't feel you can be honest, you don't feel you can be straight, you don't think you are a good vice president, you don't think you are a good dad, what you are saying to yourself and what you are saying to your son, you are always in conflict; and that's why this seems to take up so much time.

Relaxation says I can be straight, I can be honest, and I can be with you without lying all day long to myself. In that moment when you are in agreement with who you are and who the world is, time disappears and you are in this very moment, this very moment is really all that exists, but it takes that feeling of relaxation.

So first you thought there were twenty-four hours in a day, now you can almost see that I am right when I say there is forty-eight hours in a day. As an experiment, just watch yourself bullshitting with everyone you meet, even when you love them, and see how difficult it is to express yourself. And then check it out in those moments where "how you feel" and "what you say" are the same, see if there is anything in time, this time. You might discover misery takes a lot of time, but remember joy? Remember your last orgasm? Time just stands still; there you are in the moment and you can't remember how long it lasts because you cannot remember ecstasy, you cannot remember joy, and, you can't tell how long it took. So therefore when I ask you how much time did

to find all in the now, to find the whole in this." Basho

you spend yesterday alive, you would probably say, "My god, twenty-four hours and it felt like an eternity." We just have lost that quality of joy and when we did experience it, it was so fleeting because it does not take up any time. So look at yourself; obviously there are not forty-eight hours at a day and believe it or not, there are not even twenty-four hours a day. In fact there is no such thing as a day. I know I sounds crazy but this is it, right now this is it again, right now again it's just happening.

Now hold up your index finger, that's you. Now hold up the middle finger, the fuck you finger, and that's me. I know you probably want to take a punch at me because I am so fucking crazy, I spend too much time in the East, you should have stayed there, I wish I hadn't picked up this book, you are a complete idiot and I am going to punch your lights out Krishna Prem because you are such an asshole. And here is the situation; if you see yourself as the index finger and you see me as the fuck you finger and you see us as two fingers, of course we are gonna be in competition and of course you are gonna be pissed off that I have anything to say to you, that the East has any value at all, that I should have never left the West in the first place, that the West is the real world and the East is the dream world.

So here we are two fingers in conflict, I understand because when I became the fuck you finger, I was pissed off and I did want to leave the real world of America for the relaxation of the East, but what I have learned now and what I hope to express to you, is that as long as we see each other as two fingers the fight will continue but if we see each other as two fingers of one hand, this for me is the meditation. We may still have something to say to each other, you may still wanna take a swing at me, but you would be wanting to do that instead of to beat the shit out of me. You may be doing that to say, "Hey, wake up! I would love to play with you.

106

"Where is intimacy found if not in the give and take of love? Be drunken with

I would love to enjoy. You have learned too much in the East, you need balance." I am suggesting that the people from the West need balance. Balance is what we are talking about right now, what we are just sharing right now. We are just fighting right now but the concept in the East is that the higher value is in that seeing that we are two fingers of one hand. In the East we express that self as not two, in other words in the West we would love to say, "We are one" and not believe it. In the East they say, "We are not two." There is a qualitative difference; right now I am having a cup of coffee so I can't see that difference. We are two fingers of the same hand. We are not two human beings, we are one human being. We are not two human doers; we are two human beings merging into one. When you are going to become a human being instead of a human doer?

I mean basically what I am saying is that unless you take a hat off of being a vice president and leave it off, and put the hat on and be the father and when your son goes to bed take it off, and if you don't learn to take these hats off, you end up living in a crowd, your whole life is a crowd and it all gets confused; when am I a vice president and when am I a father, when am I a husband, when am I a man? You just live in a crowd and you need to take the time to throw out these people that you are living with. Even though you think all of these people are you, and basically my feeling is that every single person you have even been involved with, you are living with.

We're so lonely and so unable to be alone in the West that our parents lives inside of us, our first-grade teacher lives inside of us, our first girlfriend that kissed us on the cheek lives inside of us; our first high-school girlfriend, our first football friend, every single person we have ever met we have invited to come and live inside our mind and we never remember to say goodbye, they are

love, for love is all that exists." Rumi

all still there. It can reach to the point of madness where there is no room for you, you have invited everybody to live with you and the hotel in your mind is full and the only person that checks out is you. So I say go back into the hotel and start giving everybody their notices, start with the people you can't stand, they are really easy, you don't even mind, "Fuck you! Get out of my hotel; this is my mind and I would like to be alone for a while." And once you get rid of the people you can't stand, then take a look at the people you love. I mean basically you love when they visit, you love when they are there, you love when they are in your presence but right now you need some time, you need to go even to the people that you love and say, "Guess what, I wanna be alone now. I trust myself and I am ready to be myself, goodbye." And when you are in the area, drop in, come say hello, spend some time with me and remember to leave and for sure I am gonna remember to ask you to go.

Basically a meditation is just a clearing house of all the people that you have invited, asking them to go. Once you have asked them to go then we can start looking at career and we can start trusting that guess what, I know how to be a vice president now, I don't need to hold that thought all the time. I can just be in this moment, I know who I am, I know how to act, I trust that I have learned my job and I don't have to hold the concept of being a vice president in my mind all the time so that I am ready.

So by now you know that we are looking at the big you, the big you is the god in you. The little you is your personality, your mask face, what the Greeks call persona. What we are looking for now is to take our mask off, to be naked first of all before your very self. In a sense when you are naked, we are no longer talking about the self. We are talking about your no-self. We are shifting from the little you, the one you know so well, let's just call it your ego. Back
108

"Love should be the only way for men and women to live together. No other

to the big you, the you that existed before you were told who you are, the big you that existed before you knew who you are, before your parents even made love in order to conceive you. This is the big you. Very hard to identify with because there is no one to identify with, it's the not big you. It's a little confusing but if you keep looking, this book is to challenge you. It's gonna piss you off because I am looking for the you that does not exist. So when I say something to you that pisses you off, see if you can look further into the one in you that cannot be pissed off, the one in you that is just watching your character, your personality being pissed off. If I can piss you off, I did a fabulous job because I am pointing out that you are still identified with your ego. And eventually when I piss you off you will begin to laugh and say, "My god, he has got me again." But there is no "he" to get you. I am also looking with you. When I piss you off be clear; I, Krishna Prem, can go there too. I, Krishna Prem, can also identify with this very button that I am pushing with you. There is no problem that you have that I don't have also. I am just saying let's go beyond our problems, let's look at ourselves individually as existence, let's have some fun with Krishna Prem, let's have some fun with you. Let's laugh and say, "Thank you for finding that point of me that still itches. That I still identify, that still pisses me off, that I would like to change about myself." And let's look at it this way, let's not try and change, let's try and be. When are we going to drop being the human doer, the human personality? When are we finally going to be, once and for all, a human being? When you go inside of yourself, deep enough and you meet the god in you, you are not meeting someone else. You are meeting your own essence....

I spoke before about the zone in sport, and there is also a zone in meditation. That zone is when your personality is running and you are watching the personality run. Seeing what is essential,

ritual is needed." Osho

what you need to get through the day and knowing that it's one big cosmic joke that you can let go of your personality, let go of your ego and still get through the day, and still enjoy learning to trust this existence. Let's face it, we have all become attached to our existence, we have become attached to our bodies, to our family, to our society. And the definition of this attachment; it actually means there is no space between the real you and the play that you are involved in. You are so identified with your play, you are so identified with your family, with your religion, with your society, that there is no space to back up, to see it's just a cosmic game and that you don't need any of these crutches that you have been given by your parents and by your society. You too can be free, and by the way you are already free, you just don't know it!

Naked you are who you are, you have always been who you are, and you only are who you are. This is it, the here and now. Just take a moment to see if you can let it come in that you already are enlightened, that you already are everything you wanted to be. It's not easy, is it? I mean, say you wanna be a doctor. Being a doctor is not who you are. In other words you have got to a point where when the kid says, "When I grow up I wanna be an Indian warrior," or "I wanna be a doctor," or "I wanna be a lawyer." These are all things, these are just clothing. They are not who you are. If you wanna be a doctor become a doctor, that's great but it does not mean that you are a doctor. You are never what you think you are, you are only who you are. We go to church, we pray for an hour on a Sunday morning and then we go home and then we do everything that we did not pray for, because we have to take care of ourselves. We have no such thing as trust in our lives; we simply don't have love in our lives. What I mean by that is when is the last time you did not judge your neighbor? When is the last time you loved your neighbor? And I don't mean it in a selfish

"Do not meditate - be! Do not think that you are - be! Don't think about being -

way; I mean it in a way that we win. We win, the other person loses. When is the last time you actually did go for a win-win situation? When did that work for you last?

So instead of adding to your life "I am a doctor," "I am politician," "I am a priest," I am saying subtract from your personality. Let go of all those things that you think you are. Good-looking, ugly, funny, sad; let go of everything, let go of your personality. Begin to undress yourself. And you come upon absolutely nothing and out of this nothing begins the discovery of who you really are. For example from this nothing, from this silence instead of being a doctor, you may experience bliss. Instead of being a catholic, you may experience joy. You don't know what you are going to experience and it may even be sadness but everything you experience once you are naked comes and goes. There is no identification; this is only what is seen. Again we become a child with the name awareness. This innocence is enlightened.

Unconsciousness always repeats itself. Consciousness is brand new. In a sense meditation is warrior training. In the West we are simply told to hurry up, hurry up; this is it; you only have one life to live, you don't have time to be a witness, and you need to get involved with your life. In the East, my god, you have so many lifetimes, what's the rush? In fact, when I once explained to an Indian friend the Spanish word mañana, meaning we could do this tomorrow we don't have to hurry up, my friend told me that in the Hindi language there was no such urgent word as mañana. In India we have lifetimes and lifetimes. In America we have only this lifetime; hurry up! I guess what I am trying to say is somewhere in the middle of this is it, we only have one lifetime and you have forever, why do anything at all? You are just going to come back

you are!" Sri Ramana Maharshi

again into another body and make the same mistakes again. I guess the middle way is to be here and now.

One of my favorite moments with Osho was when he was talking about the known, the unknown, and the unknowable. The known, you just simply know it. For some unknown reason you just know. And then there is the unknown and that is you go to university and you find out, you go to school, you ask your parents, "I don't know this, it's above the physical plane, can you help me understand this, it's of interest to me." And yes the unknown then becomes the known. And then there is the third category, the first being the known, the second being the unknown, the third category is the unknowable, that which you cannot know. Again in the East we say not knowing is the most intimate experience you can have. But I think clarity about who you are is when you can see these three things, the known, the unknown and the unknowable, and have them be true for you. Know what you know, find out what you need to know and then relax knowing that you will never know the unknowable and it feels really good. And one of the things Osho said about this, is that even if you knew the unknowable, what difference would it make? Does not make any difference at all, so instead of killing yourself trying to know the unknowable, just relax. Relax into knowing that it does not make a difference, because the most intimate experience you can have is to relax with the unknowable. It is not something you need to know. The enlightened man cannot see himself. He can only see what is going on. The seer cannot be seen, the seer sees. So you can look at who you are to existence, but you can't look at who you are to your own eyes. You are the seen, you cannot see you. You need to begin to trust it, to embrace it, to love it. This is who you are so why not love it?

"The only difference between a wise man and a fool is that the wise man knows

Buddha always reminds us that happiness is letting-go. This is also called in the East uncaused joy. Can I prove this to you? No I can't. But I can tell you that if you look inside for the answer you won't find it. What you may find, the deeper you look inside, is that the question actually disappears and once there is no question, there is no answer. There was never any answer, but there has always been a question because you haven't been yourself in a really long time. Become yourself, become intimate and the question disappears and the answer is that which you don't know and that which you can embrace. This is what we call meditation; A god with no name.

When you find the roots into yourself, into your no-self, you also can feel your wings expanding. We call this in the East roots and wings. When a master looks into your eyes, he is also seeing if your feet are grounded. He is also seeing if you are waving in the wind, totally vulnerable and yet grounded at the same time, completely at ease with the unknowable. It's almost like in the East enlightenment is presented as an unidentified flying object, and in the West this object is identified as god. So in the East we have no god, in the West we have a god. Never the two shall meet unless they meet in you. It's not easy to stop looking through your identification and just to see through your being. There is no god other than life itself. And when I say that I also am saying never obey and never listen to me, I don't know shit. Sounds good though and I like what I am saying, but don't take my answer to your question.

Osho once wrote a book called Get Out of Your Own Way. This does not mean to space-out, to leave your body. This means to be present, to be a presence. Intelligent people know other people, enlightened people know themselves. This is to paraphrase from Lao Tzu. Buddha said the same thing when he said, "Be a light

he's playing." Fritz Perls

unto yourself." It wasn't until Osho got here that someone had the courage to say, "Be a joke unto yourself." I hope I am not confusing you too much; it may be I am confusing you because you are confused, and it may be that I am confusing you because I am confused. It's the eternal Zen paradox.

But just to lighten up the situation here I remember I once sent a joke in to Osho, a really bad joke and he told it. He liked it so I will tell it to you. You'll probably remember it, it may be one of the first jokes you ever heard:

How did the Fagawi Indian tribe get its name?

It was late at night and the young warrior comes to wake up the chief and he says to the chief, "I absolutely think we are lost. I don't know which way to go. I am a chief but I just have no idea." And the chief said, "Meditate on it and if you can't find out where the hell we are, wake me in the morning." So first thing in the morning the young warrior woke the chief and he said, "I am just totally confused." and the chief gets out of the bed in a huff and a puff, mounts his pony, rides off to the edge of the desert, shades his eyes with his hand and looks out and he says, "Where the fuck are we?" and that's how the Fagawi Indian tribe got its name.

Stupid joke, Osho liked it. I think it's a stupid joke but when the master likes the stupid joke I need to share it with you. It's all about sharing. I always like that simple little expression "I like your problems." Because when you like your problems they are not problems at all. They are simply situations to be transcended.

When I got back from India for the very first time, I asked my friends if they wanted to meditate with me, to be with me, more often than not that my friends said, "Are you crazy? That's too dangerous. Let's drop acid instead." Sex and drugs and rock 'n'

114

roll. How about breathing, tantra, music and silence? Osho reminds us that meditation brings two things. It brings wisdom and it brings freedom. These are the two flowers that grow out of meditation. When you become silent, utterly silent beyond the mind, two flowers bloom in you. You become liberated. Meditation is the key to liberation, to freedom, to wisdom, to you. It's worth it. It does not cost money to be yourself, you don't need a religion to be yourself, and you don't need a post-graduate degree to be yourself. You can be yourself and have a post-graduate degree. You can be yourself and have a religion. You can be yourself and be wise. That's who you are, enjoy.

We are talking a lot about meditation, maybe because I am a man and in a sense meditation is the masculine way and love is the feminine way. Meditation means the capacity to be absolutely alone and love means the capacity to be absolutely together. Both do the same work. Osho reminds us that on both paths the ego disappears. Love means rejoicing in relatedness and meditation means rejoicing in solitude and aloneness. In a sense you have to see which path is more suited to you. And not only that you have to see if right now the path that suits me is still suited to me. In other words at certain points maybe love is your path, at other points maybe meditation is your path.

I wanna say here I met a man called Osho that I fell in love with and this became my path. But I am not at all saying that you need a guru. What I am saying is that as a man who has himself for a lawyer has a fool for a client, so you might say that a man who has himself for a guru has a fool for a disciple.

But I can honestly say to you that whether you want a guru or need a guru or prefer to walk alone, as long as you are not a fool and at the same time have the ability to laugh at yourself because

for all your actions." Nepalese good luck mantra

you are a fool, you are at home. If being with a guru takes you further into your ego, if being alone takes you further into your ego, maybe you want to get on the ground with a small child and just crawl, crawl and see everything as if it's brand new. Or maybe you want to go to the Himalayas and look for the oldest, longest beard and ask him, "How could I regain my innocence?" In fact you might in this moment in time ask her how you could regain your innocence. Life is not only known to men, it's not only known to women. Life is, and from this comes men and women. Men and women don't come into it; it comes to men and women. There is a great expression: does a dog have consciousness?

This is one of the oldest Zen koans in the world and I wanna tell you right now that I don't know, but I can honestly say to you that consciousness has the dog. Consciousness has you. Dog is god spelled backwards. Life has you right by the balls. Whether you have balls or not, it has you by the balls. Or to put it another way, it has you by the no-balls. Balls and no-balls appear from a tennis game called life. It's coming out to you; you are not going into it. Consciousness has you and you have the ability to have consciousness. This is what we call the flow. Life is you and you are life and there are no breaks. It's a one-ness, you have returned to who you are. You have become the source again. This is the height of meditation.

Once you are enlightened, you know there is no such thing as enlightened, there is no you to become enlightened. The you that you thought would become enlightened has disappeared into that very moment. So in fact there is before enlightenment and there is beyond enlightenment, but the actual enlightenment disappears in the very moment that enlightenment happens to you. When enlightenment happens to you, you are no longer, so there is, in a sense, no one to become enlightened.

116

Why did the Buddhist coroner get fired? Because he'd always recorded the

I don't mean to drive you crazy. I don't mean to suggest that there are two of you; the you that is existence and the you that is personality. In fact, there is only life, there is only you, there is only God. However, without training to know this, by the time we are three years old, we have been told everything but that. The witness is the foundation of meditation. The witness is consciousness. Basically there is no meaning in the world, all meaning is the very center of your being, the world is simply noise, there is no music – life is like a game of chess, all the kings, queens and pawns go in the same box at the end, so there is no meaning. The only meaning is how you play the game. Every seven years every cell in your body comes and goes. You might look at baby pictures of yourself and not recognize who you are. A risk at twenty-eight is like a walk in the park, yet that same risk might have you crippled by fear if you took it in your fifties, and this is what is meant by life is a river flowing.

You are the center of the cyclone. What you identify with is simply a storm called by your name and until you know who the witness is, that place in you that is nameless and formless and all awareness, you'll always think life is a drama and not a cosmic comedy. And we're not talking about sitting in lotus heaven, or moving to the Himalayas without your dentist, which is a fear of every meditator that believes the saints. It simply means that you can watch the movies you are starring in without committing suicide moment-to-moment. The only moment that is true is the one that flows out of you when you are beyond fear and expectation. So be alert, don't wonder if the girl is going to kiss you, just be in the moment, because there is no better way of attracting a French kiss. There's nothing sexier than resting in yourself and if you don't believe me, I wouldn't read any further in this book, just give it away. And if you do believe me, don't kill

cause of death as 'birth.' Veda

me just because you don't want to commit suicide; it's a wild fuckin' ride.

The only way we can really meet each other is when we are naked, naked in the sense that you and I are in bed together without our personalities getting in the way. This is the true meaning of tantra, that the oneness in me meets the oneness in you. I'd love to tell you that this makes us soul mates, but as far as I'm concerned soul mates is the mind dreaming about love, I'm talking about you & I returning to who we are, to the point where neither one of us exists.

When I bought Geetam we went to the local hotel bar to celebrate. As you know my real-estate agent, Ron, and I had become very close, so in fact I only kept half his commission check and he was taking his remaining half of the commission and flying off to India to meet Osho. His name became Anubuddha. He no longer sells real-estate. He is the founder of Arun Touch and he's a world-famous bodywork teacher. He started life as a conman and now he's a vegan. An alchemical transformation. At that point he was much more worldly than me, and he bought the first round of drinks, and of course being the perfect gentleman I bought the next round. In the high desert of California having a drink is like having a drink on an airplane. Quickly I became inebriated. I excused myself and went to the men's room, went into the little stall and my body fell to the ground. The beauty of the story is that I didn't, and I simply said to my body to not be such a dramatic drunk because I don't want to spend my whole life in the men's room. I was very amused that my body staggered to its feet and was able to do its business without a splash. This is not the best example in my life for suggesting to you that you are not your body, but I think it's one you can relate to.

"A real friend is someone who walks in when the rest of the world walks out."

I had this experience before, during basic training in the U.S. Army at Fort Polk, Louisiana. You may remember it because it is often referred to in military circles as the armpit of the nation. I was nominated for Soldier of the Cycle and at the same time I was confronting a court martial. In my boots and full army fatigues I would run for hours, singing the song, *Up the hill! Down the hill! How far? All the way! Airborne Rangers!* I noticed that after eight kilometers my body began to run without me. I would just sit on my own shoulder and go into cruise-control. If I wasn't so angry with the U.S. Army at the time, I might have called this being in the zone.

I first met Osho on Valentine's Day in 1973 at a meditation camp in the Indian desert. At night, I slept on the ground just outside the room where he was staying, and, as I recall, the mosquitoes that kept me company were bigger than my consciousness. I'd just arrived in India after my five-year fight with the army about Vietnam.

In the morning, Osho sat in a chair just in front of me, dressed in a simple white robe. My first thought was: how can a man have such so much strength and lightness at the same time? I remember instantly falling in love with him while not exactly feeling great about myself. My dark side, my inner secret, was killing me. Out of the blue, Osho looked at me and said, "The revolution is inside yourself."

Up until that moment the revolution had been outside. The enemy was outside, the army was outside, my girlfriends were outside, life was outside, and I hated it all. And when Osho said that, it was like something went off in my head. I knew that I could work on myself, that I could drop the hate I had toward life. I could drop the hate I had for myself.

St. Francis of Assi

"A man of peace is not a pacifist; a man of peace is simply a pool of silence. He pulsates a new kind of energy into the world, he sings a new song. He lives in a totally new way, his very way of live is that of grace, that of prayer, that of compassion. "Whomsoever he touches, he creates more love-energy. The man of peace is creative. He is not against war, because to be against anything is to be at war. He is not against war; he simply understands why war exists. And out of that understanding he becomes peaceful. Only when there are many people who are pools of peace, silence, understanding, will the war disappear."

Zen: The Path of Paradox, Vol II, Osho

There are two u's in the word guru. The first u is the you, I call the capitol you, it is existence itself. The second u is called the little you, that is your daily life. That's who you've been told you are. By your parents, by your society, and later on as you've become more hypnotized, by yourself.

So, what happens for me, and happened to me, is that my little you became my boss. Because when I looked into the little u, into the mirror of life, all I could see is my ego. My ego, for me, is not real, anymore. But when it was real, it represented all that I learned until the age of three, even as I was conceived to be a human being. Mommy and Daddy talked to me incessantly about what they would like me to be and do and feel.

In the first three years before you learn the word "no," all you do is take in all these great concepts of how fabulous life can be if you listen to Mommy and Daddy. By the time you learn to say "no," because you can talk back, it's too late. So what I mean is when you look at yourself in the mirror and you say, "Who am I?"

"Meditation keeps me grounded. It doesn't mean I am perfect. It means I have

you really look only as far as your ego, only as far as your protection.

So what am I saying? Like every great teacher you have ever met, every coach, just throw away your ego. Well, it's not so easy to throw away your ego. Your ego has done a fabulous job helping you to protect yourself against everybody that does not look and feel like you. So I say, "No! No! No! Let's really get into our egos." Let's blow up this identity so big, so really, really big: I am the greatest. I am Mohammed Ali. I can kick his ass from the one end of America to the other end of Zimbabwe. But once that ego is tremendously big, at least what happened for me is that I was able to see through my ego, because there were holes now. In other words, if you make the ego really small and tight, it looks solid, it looks real, it looks like a great box. Always gives you the right answer, always tells you how to take care of yourself, always tells you to win. But when we blow up this ego really, really big, it begins to get less real. The ego appears in the big U instead of me thinking it's my whole life. And we begin to see through it. My feeling is that if you can go with me on this, and let your ego be tremendously big, to the point where you almost feel like a fairy in the eyes of your ego, you make it really, really big. Then you can see through it. And then you begin to see the real you, the first u of the guru. You as existence.

And once you can see that you are existence, you can start to see your ego as wholly threatened, and begin to self-destruct, and begin to fall down, begin to die. It was never really real in the first place. It was only because you could not see yourself as the god in you that you failed to live up to it, as existence promised, as celebrating this very lifetime.

the guts to look at my life and enjoy it more." Batul

Now the play begins. The play that we are really here to enjoy, called the cosmic play. You see yourself as existence itself. And you act according to the real you instead of your ego.

Very, very interesting times. In meditation times we call this awareness. When you begin to see yourself and the god in you, you begin to cut away this ego, through awareness. And what do you end up with? You still end up with you as a character. You still end up with you as the small you. You still end up as the guy who gets up and has to do this day, totally. But with that support, it becomes what is known in the East as a leela, a game. You play the game to the best of your ability.

Now what most people say they feel in meditation is, "Wow! I began to meditate, I'm going to start treating people well, and I'm going to lose the game. The more I share, the more I lose." Well, of course, in abundance, the more you share, the more you gain.

Of course when you begin to meditate, you also begin to fall apart. Because here you always were acting like an individual, and now when you begin to meditate, you realize you are not an individual. We all are one. We are not a forest, we are a tree and everyone else is a tree. So you begin to be able to see that the tree is from the forest. You begin to see yourself as unique instead of part of a government.

To me governments are really simple. They say let's all drive on the left-hand side of the street when we are in Europe, except when we are in England. But let us all drive on the left-hand side of the street otherwise we are all going to have accidents. And I am going to put out the trash on Mondays and Thursdays. But governments tend to get excited and then they start to tell you who you are and that has always been my difficulty with authority. I

"Many a man has fallen in love with a girl in a light so dim he would not have

don't want my government to tell me who I am. I want them to tell me how we can best serve each other and help each other, but I don't want them to tell me who I am. No one can tell me who I am.

Often times I'm just a little crazy.

Now before I go into the big you, who you are possibly just meeting in this very moment, I don't want to say that you are the god that created the universe, that you are omnipotent, omniscient, and even that you are intelligent. I'm just saying that we are all god. We are children of god if you prefer. We are all existence if you prefer.

I love this little story: how do you make God laugh? You tell him you have a plan. So our little u asks what can we do in future to have a better life? And we make a plan. God is simply laughing at us when we hit the wall and our plans just fall apart.

And the same is true if you ask God what is the past? He also laughs. So very often this is what we mean by being here now. We are saying there is no past and there is no future. Or, we like to say the future is the incomplete experience of the past.

When you have a thought at night, right before you go to bed, very often you probably notice that when you wake up, it is also your first thought. Time is often just an incomplete experience. You just didn't have the guts to move, totally, so that time does not exist to be here now.

I relate to friends more than thoughts, so my mind is full of every friend and family member I ever met, which may look sweet and loving except I forgot to ask them to leave me alone. Osho hinted to me that I was not even present in my own life because the

chosen a suit by it." Maurice Chevalier

only one that checked out of my mind was me. He added that his Kundalini meditation is a perfect way to shake up my past and ask everyone to leave including all the gals I loved and lost.

OSHO® KUNDALINI MEDITATION™ is by far my favorite meditation. I have lead this meditation all over the world including the OSHO International Meditation Resort until I was relieved of my duties when to add intensity to this meditation, I announced that the meditation resort was closing and that this would be the very last time we would be meditating together. Everyone present threw themselves into the fray with reckless abandon... except that is eleven Taiwanese friends who didn't understand my American English and left the OSHO Auditorium in tears... my heartfelt apologies were not accepted and I was sent to my room without dinner. Without further ado, I suggest you follow the instructions to the tee, always remembering that your house is on fire... in other words, be total.

This meditation lasts for one hour and has four stages, three with music, and the last without.

Kundalini acts like an energetic shower, softly shaking you free of your day and leaving you refreshed and mellow.

First Stage: 15 minutes
Be loose and let your whole body shake, feeling the energies moving up from your feet. Let go everywhere and become the shaking. Your eyes may be open or closed.

"Allow the shaking; don't do it. Stand silently, feel it coming and when your body starts trembling, help it but don't do it. Enjoy it, feel blissful about it, allow it, receive it, welcome it, but don't will it. "If you force it will become an exercise, a bodily, physical

124

exercise. Then the shaking will be there but just on the surface; it will not penetrate you. You will remain solid, stone-like, rock-like within. You will remain the manipulator, the doer, and the body will just be following. The body is not the question – you are the question. When I say shake, I mean your solidity, your rock-like being should shake to the very foundations so that it becomes liquid, fluid, melts, flows. And when the rock-like being becomes liquid, your body will follow. Then there is no shake, only shaking. Then nobody is doing it; it is simply happening. Then the doer is not."

Second Stage: 15 minutes
Dance, any way you feel, letting the whole body move as it wishes. Again, your eyes can be open or closed.

Third Stage: 15 minutes
Close your eyes and be still, sitting or standing, observing, witnessing, whatever is happening inside and out.

Fourth Stage: 15 minutes
Keeping your eyes closed, lie down and be still.

You can download the music for this meditation or order the music on CD from www.osho.com

about events going badly. Let the lover be." Rumi

Chapter 5

Maturity: The Responsibility of Being Oneself

"This rose flower contains all the rose flowers of the past; and if you can understand, let me say, it contains all the future flowers also. This is just one flower representing all the flowers of the past and future. We are here; in this moment the whole existence converges. All the past and all the future converges in this moment. This moment is the bridge between the past and the future. In you, everything is meeting right now. If you can become aware, then you are the whole existence this very moment."

Come Follow To You, Vol 4, Osho

Wow! How easy it is to think, "I am the body." Why is this so? I think for those of us who grow up in the West, it's because there's so much emphasis on the physical and the material in our lives. Naturally, we think we are this body and that life lasts only as long the body lives. While in the East they think, "I am not the body" and more often than not say, "I am the soul that resides within it, or something else beyond."

It's interesting that many people have experienced the phenomenon of leaving their body, or standing outside their body, which seems to suggest that they are not the body. Others meanwhile, have experienced doing things but feeling like they're not really doing it, not that someone else is, but that another part of them is running the show. So, if we are able to go beyond the body and watch what it is doing, then who are we?

It's easy to say the words, "I am not the body," but really how many people don't get upset when you tell them they've put on

126

"When women are depressed, they eat or go shopping. Men invade another

weight or they're going bald, or don't perk up delightedly when you tell them they've lost weight or look gorgeously sexy today? Not that many. I can say, "I am not my body" but if you punch me in the nose, I'm probably going to feel like I am my nose for a while, at least until the sensation wears off. It's so easy to get identified with this body, to either be pissed off with it when it's suffering pain, or happy with it when it's experiencing pleasure. But just because my body feels things, does that mean it's who I am?

See this is where both Western and Eastern thinking falls short. "I am the body" implies because my body is here, I exist. "I am not the body" implies that my body is here, because I exist. Both East and West have a piece of the puzzle but neither has the whole picture. Just because we experience having a body, doesn't mean we are limited only to this body. And just because we exist beyond the body, doesn't mean we are not this body also. In my opinion, it would be more accurate to say, "Gee, I'm the body!" and "Gee, I'm beyond!"

So, we've talked about our own body, but what about other bodies, namely other people? How often do we get caught up in thinking that others are extensions of us, that others define us?

Say for example, someone in our family gets into big trouble; we might think they reflect badly on us. Say our best friend turns up wearing something totally geeky; we might not want to stand close to them. Or we take our prized partner out with us to meet the boss and they fart during dinner, then we might just want to dig a big hole and climb into it! Conversely, if our best friend just won an Academy Award, we might feel really, really proud.

127

country. It's a whole different way of thinking." Elayne Boosler

And I notice we do this with people we are close to, especially with our friends, girlfriends, boyfriends, partners, husbands and wives. Somehow, we get all wrapped up in them and then think they represent us. It's as if we extend our i-dentity to include them. And it's easy to tell when it's happening, because usually we feel either proud or embarrassed. But are you the people you relate with? Are you all the things they do? Are you your solid relationship, your rocky marriage or your string of affairs? Do your gf's, bf's, friends and family, say anything about you?

You know, some of us are more body-oriented and some of us are more mind-oriented. Hence, some of us are more likely to think we are the body, while some of us are more likely to think we are the mind. My god, this opens up a whole new can of worms! Some of us might identify more with what we have or do, while some of us might identify more with what we think or feel. We may see ourselves as our intellect or intuition, our knowledge or our IQ, our education or our qualifications. We may pride ourselves in being a fabulous philosopher, a mad professor, a technical whiz kid, or a gifted psychic or medium… or a large or a small! Or what about just plain street-wise, savvy or shrewd?

Someone once said, "I think therefore I am" and it sounds so profound, so noble that the whole Western world has based its identity on it. But, "I think therefore I am" is bullshit. "I think therefore I am" says that because the mind exists therefore so do I, when in truth it's the other way round, I exist and therefore so does the mind. "I think therefore I am" is like watching a movie and believing the movie is real and that the projector exists only because of the movie. The reality is however that the movie is only showing, because the projector exists. So, perhaps a more accurate statement would be, "I am therefore I think." U exist whether you

"I can remember when the air was clean and sex was dirty." George Burns think or not, and who you are precedes your thinking and fortunately, is not dependent on it.

Athletes often bump into meditation. The word zone is becoming very, very big now and I think that they think the zone is real. For me it happened in running a few times where after running for about eight miles all of a sudden the body begin to run all by itself. It's almost like you leave the body and just let the body carry on. No effort, just the flow. I am not a professional athlete, I am not even a great athlete, I am just having fun in my body and often, at any level there is a zone, at every level. Say in tennis, which I play a lot, even at the D level in Europe or what would probably be just the second or third level in America in tennis; it often happens that all of a sudden you know how to play the game. The game knows how to play you, all of a sudden the racket is back, the forehand drives, you are going cross-court, getting ready for the return of the energy from your opposite partner. All of a sudden everything is working and the mind disengages. You know there are great athletes, it's easy to see. You see Boris Becker in his day at Wimbledon, literally flying through the air, racket ready and you can see his zone. Sometimes watching a great athlete you can be in the zone and you can see he is totally centered, totally steady. He is not flying through the air; his body is flying through the air. So for me often times in sports it's just an aberration, every sport requires a different muscle group to be applied. So sometimes you are talking to your body about playing tennis. And once you learn that, you need to drop out of the way and let your body play tennis, that you are not really that necessary. I like to think of it as ready, set and let go. I don't know if it's true in every country but in America, as children, if we were going to run a race, we'd say go ready, set, go. And in sport as far as the zone is concerned, how I like to see it is ready, set, let-go.

"Today we have analog teachers teaching digital kids." Abhijat

Get your body ready, get your mind set and then get out of your own way, let-go, trust. I think one of the beautiful things about sport whether it be the mathematics of playing tennis, or being a football player, it's about getting ready, using your mind to explain to your body what we are going to do now and then just get the fuck out of town. Just relax and play. And the more you can relax and play, the more the quality of the experience goes way up. I think the problem that a lot of people have is sometimes they really play a sport well and now they have gone for a job and they don't know how to take the let-go from one experience called, say, playing tennis or playing football and use it in the marketplace when they have a job. But the same rules apply, you need to get ready, you need to get set and you need to trust. You need to let-go. It's a very difficult lesson to learn and my feeling is if you can let-go as an athlete, you can let-go as a businessman. I think passion is the word here also, if you are not passionate about what you are doing it's really difficult to be ready enough to let-go to be in the moment.

Let's look at dancing for example, as sport, because many young people love to dance. So there's two ways; one is to dance your heart out as if you don't exist at all, just disappearing into the dance. That's one meditation technique. Another meditation technique would be to watch your body dance. So you need to know for yourself which technique works for you and the best way to find out is put on some music now, do a little dance, get down tonight.

Does it really matter if the dancer disappears in the dance or the witness sees his body disappearing through dancing, does it make a difference? Whatever works, whatever works. I hope I am not making you take life too seriously. Sometimes this book seems a little serious but I love the expression that no one has ever been

130

credited for, because no one knows who said it first, probably some ordinary person just having a cigarette after making love said, "Never take life seriously, nobody gets out alive anyway."

Just bringing up cigarette smoking, I will never forget, I was reading The National Enquirer, one of my bibles, when all of a sudden there was a joke about meditation. Very simply two monks are sitting with the master and they both enjoy sneaking out and having a cigarette. They are feeling guilty about it and they felt maybe they would discuss this with the master. So one monk asked the master, "Can I smoke while I meditate?" And the master said, "Absolutely not." And the other boy took a moment, took a deep breath and he said to the master, "Can I meditate while I smoke?" And the master said, "Certainly you can." So right there I had a moment of meditation and delight, thank you to the editors of the The National Enquirer.

And then I heard another dirty joke which I like very much because every kid's meditation is this; "Which came first, the chicken or the egg?" I was a little kid when someone first asked me that question. It really threw me for a loss. And I just heard the answer, "When a chicken and an egg were in bed together and they just made love and the chicken lights up a cigarette and the egg says I guess we now know who came first!" Friends would often ask Osho about smoking and he would say, "It really does not make a big difference if you smoke, you probably just live a couple of years less than if you don't smoke, but it does not really make a difference." Then he would chuckle and of course all through his Resort we have smoking temples so that people that do smoke have a place to go without feeling guilty. Because guilt will keep you smoking that is pretty sure, but you would always say, if pressed, that you try to smoke with awareness. To take your cigarette pack, to look at it, to see what it's made of, to feel it, to

131

take a cigarette slowly out of the pack and put it to your lips, light the cigarette and feel the tobacco smoke going down your lungs – how does that feel? Does it feel like a breath of fresh air? Does it feel dirty? Does it disturb your quality of life at all? And he would never give any answer but more and more people would be going to the smoking temple and not having a cigarette while they were there, but they'd be smelling the passive smoke. You know mediators often don't smoke but if they do smoke they smoke passionately, that this is their very last cigarette while they are here. Who am I right now doing this cigarette? Often times someone would just sneak off into a corner and have a cigarette in order just to have a moment with themselves, and it's kind of cute because in a way meditation is being intimate with oneself. So I don't smoke personally but if I did I would enjoy it also.

Maybe what I am saying is that awareness helps you make the same mistake only once. Say if you are a smoker and you enjoy smoking, I don't know what to say to you but I do actually identify a lot with someone who smokes at one period of his life, uses awareness to realize that the body is not enjoying this experience health-wise and drops the experience. I think in meditation often times we say that an intelligent person only makes the same mistake once. The French have a great expression, "If you make the same mistake twice..." in fact the way they say it is, "If you get married twice, you are going to get married three times." So if you keep repeating the mistake through unawareness, only awareness can call this to your attention.

Osho always used to say an enlightened man never makes the same mistake once. Basically you never step into the same river twice because the river is always moving. I love the story about the boy that was walking on Malibu beach in California, just pulling on a cigarette and deep in thought and totally upset with himself;

132

"Sex goes downwards, love goes upwards, prayer goes nowhere. It is a state

his girlfriend just left him, he'd just got fired from work, it could not have been worse. The only thing he has is the sun beating on his face and taking a long drag of a cigarette, just kicking his feet in the sand, disgusted with life and my god, he kicks a magic lamp and the genie comes out of the magic lamp and says, "Thank you, thank you, thank you. I have been stuck in the magic lamp for 400 years and I know, kind sir, that you were told that you would get three wishes from the genie, but to be honest with you I am exhausted after all that time in that little lamp. I am gonna take a swim, I am only here to grant you one wish." And the guy looks at the genie in disbelief but he has heard the story before and he says to the genie, "Well, I am afraid of flying but what I would really love to do is drive to Hawaii, to get away from California." The genie said, "Well, I have been asleep for 400 years but if you think that I can build a bridge from here to Hawaii... even though I have been asleep for 400 years, I am pretty sure that there is not an engineer that could show me how to build that bridge for you. Give me one last chance, give me one last question that I can help you with and make it fast, I want to get out of here." So the guy said, "I tell you what, I don't understand women. If you can help me understand women that would be my one wish." And the genie scratches his head and he looks at the guy and he says, "Would you like to be the bridge to be two lanes or four lanes?"

I mean really, does anybody give a shit about meditation? Don't we really wanna understand the opposite sex, would you not really rather write a great book on men understanding women and women understanding men? Don't we feel all so terribly lonely and unhappy with just being alone? Will meditation really satisfy me so that I can just sit here in my aloneness and do nothing at all and be happy? Now that is a very good question, can I do anything for you when I write this book? Have I learned anything about

133

of being. You simply are." Osho

meditation and being alone? Let's look at this. To be honest I would be lying to you if I told you I had the answer to this eternal question. I know that we are all one but after that I don't know much. Women remain an absolute mystery to me. But one of the things I am working with in writing this book, interestingly enough to me, is about the Buddhist experience called "Not-knowing is the most intimate experience." And I only bring this up because as a man, when I say I don't know, often times what I am saying is please ask me tomorrow because tomorrow I will know the answer. And when a woman says to me, "I don't know," it doesn't seem to create the future. For me not-knowing creates the future. For many of the women that I know, not knowing is ok as long as breakfast tastes good. I don't know how to explain it in any other way except that there does seem to be a pretty big difference between men and women. I absolutely know there is a difference, I know that the deeper we go into ourselves, there isn't a difference but that is certainly not a great answer.

Life is a mystery to be lived, not a problem to be solved. I will never forget one time I was in love with a girl and what broke us up was she fell in love with another master, not Osho. And of course we got into comparison and nothing ruins a relationship more than comparison; your guru is better than my guru. Our relationship was going down the drain quickly. I was pretty much in love and remember that I was driving her home for the last time. I will never forget we got caught in a traffic jam and we were just crawling along and I remember saying to myself, "There is nowhere else that I wanna be right now than in this traffic jam." You know that's what love can do; it's bigger than the traffic jam. You can go standstill pace on a sixty mile-an-hour freeway and be happy as a pig in shit. That's what I call love and that's what I call

"From the smallest blade of grass to the biggest star, everybody is needed,

abundance. Another day that traffic jam would have just driven me up the wall, today it was perfect.

Basically Osho spoke everyday that I have known him for about two hours a day when he spoke, and then he would go into silence. After silence he would really enjoy speaking about god and the self and the no self, he really was a brilliant man when it came to discussing meditation and he just did not need any notes to speak for those two hours. The only time he ever used his notes seriously is when he wanted to tell a joke. In other words for me, what I was watching was how seriously he took telling a joke well. And also the jokes were about the only thing where I knew the punch line before he said it! I've always enjoyed a good joke, just like you, so I have heard a lot of jokes, and Osho knew and always reminded us that most of the jokes actually came out of America where I came from. The most fun I had with Osho was actually sending jokes to him. I rarely asked him questions about the pursuit of happiness, but I did give him answers, meaning I sent him a lot of jokes. And I would make the jokes that I sent to him very complicated and he would really actually read the jokes that I sent to him many times, and I could actually close my eyes and be in the moment with him, if you know what I mean. So one night I was sitting in the front row with my eyes closed and all of a sudden I got excited because he read a joke that I sent to him. The beauty of this story is that I sent him this joke all the time because he never told it and I couldn't understand why not, because it was such a great joke. Then another week would go by and I would send him the joke again and then I decided not to send him any more jokes until he told this particular joke. Finally one night he told the joke and you might have heard it but I want to say it now because it was really cute:

equally needed. There is no hierarchy in existence." Osho

A boy goes to temple and he says to God, "You know, I have been coming to temple my whole life as far back as I can remember, and I have always prayed and I have always been a good person and I have always followed the bible and basically nothing good happened from it. So I will tell you what God, I want some actual proof that you are listening to me and paying attention and serving me because it's not about just me serving you. I wanna be served back. So I will tell you what I am gonna do. Unless I win the lottery in the next year I am going to drop the church." And lo and behold the year passes and the boy is sitting in temple and he says to God, "Well, this is it God, you never did anything to prove it to me and I did not win the lottery. That's it; I am never coming back to temple again." And all of a sudden the whole roof of the temple completely rises, thunder cracks through the sky, the clouds open up and here is God with his bearded face and he looks down at the boy and he says, "My god, at least meet me half way – buy a lottery ticket!"

Now Osho would of course have been a better comedian every day as he got older; he did not laugh at his own jokes but he always smiled when he heard laughter from the audience and everybody loved this joke. It has got that great Jewish humor with this punch-line and a little bit of reality thrown in. And I really loved it because the whole time Osho read word for word, every single word that I had sent to him including the names of the characters in the joke. And this was the most fun I had with him because to be honest I was new to meditation, new to love, new to devotion, new to trust and every word was brand new because I did not have a lot of experience at that time. But I knew a good joke when I heard one and I loved sending it to him. One of the first jokes I ever sent to him, which I thought was terrible, he actually

136

"Man is not meant to crawl and creep on the earth. He has the capacity to fly

liked very much and you probably remember it because that joke is as old as a joke can be. And the joke is:

What did the sadist say when the masochist said, "Hit me?"

The sadist said, "No."

Laughter is a real prayer. It's a real show of gratitude. Laughing at life, laughing at death; laughing is. You know I am old enough now where many of my friends are not well in their bodies and when I can, I always give them a little five-dollar sculpture of the laughing buddha called Hotei. And Hotei was a man that was very well loved and had a great sense of humor. When he died, he knew that people would be sad and he wondered how they could possibly be sad when all he has been showing them is how delightful life is and how delightful death is. But sadness is always there at funerals it seems like. So what he did was he packed his body with fireworks, and as everybody began to cry when his body began to burn the fireworks went off, and all through the funeral pyre it was just one firework going off after another and everybody got that he was celebrating his own death and they began to laugh and celebrate with him. I know this is a very difficult concept for us in the West that anybody would wanna celebrate death, and I am not suggesting to you that I will be able to celebrate my own death. I am just saying why do we take it so seriously? Why do we think it is such a disappointing experience; if we enjoy life, why can't we enjoy death? Are we really our bodies, are we really our minds, aren't we bigger than that? It's up to you and I can't really answer for you. So here's another joke I sent to Osho:

Abe is living in Malibu, a very, very wealthy boy and he has just always given himself to people; they needed a new temple, he built a temple. It's a Sunday afternoon and he is relaxing at home

137

and the waves are storming in and there is thunder in the air. The Fire Department rings on his door bell and the guy says, "Abe, we are evacuating the area, it looks like there is gonna be a huge wave coming into Malibu, a tsunami, and we would like you to come with us Abe, you have been a great man and a great support to the community and we would like to save you." And Abe says very gently, "In my hour of need only God can save me." And the Fire Department just leaves. Now we have a Coast Guard cutter coming into the shore, "Abe, please come with us. The tsunami is coming, the huge wave is coming. You need to evacuate." And Abe says, "In my hour of need only God can help me." Now Abe is on his roof and the Air Force helicopter comes, just wind is blowing, "Abe please, this is it. You have got to come with us now." And Abe says, "In my hour of need…" and the helicopter takes off and the tsunami wave comes and crushes Abe's house, kills Abe, he's soaking wet, and he knocks at the door of heaven. St. Peter says, "Abe, Abe we have been waiting for you. Come in." And then Abe comes in and he is sitting in front of God but he is not looking at God. So God said, "Abe, I have been waiting for you for so long. Why are you taking life so seriously, why aren't you delighted to see me?" And Abe said, "Where were you God, in my hour of need?" And God said, "Are you kidding? I sent the Fire Department, I sent the Navy, I sent the Air Force…."

Osho loved that joke and so do I.

Isn't it true that we all think we are special? The last thing that God whispered in your ear before you were born is, "Abe, you are special." That word special can really cripple us. It makes us feel absolutely separate, we always feel, deep down, that we're better than everybody else. And that special-ness creates separateness and that separateness creates us actually being enemies. We are one. Better to say we are all ordinary. But these two jokes that I

138

just told you, I guess I told them because I am so excited that Osho spoke them so exactly. They are great jokes but they are all these jokes that indicate that god is outside of us, but one of the most beautiful stories I have ever heard was:

God was finished with creation. He'd created man and women and so many animals and so many trees that everybody just bothering could I be as tall as that other tree, could I be as beautiful as that flower, could I be as beautiful as that flower, could my tits be bigger, my penis longer? Everybody had requests and the guy was really getting bothered, he loved what he created but nobody seemed satisfied. So he decided to get out of town, to go and seek some peace. And he was sitting with his wise man and he said, "Where could I go to get away from all these questions? I don't have the answers for these people, they are gonna have to find out for themselves that they are beautiful unto themselves." And he said to the wise man, "How about if I build myself a house on the moon?" And the wise man said, "Man is so curious that I can't imagine that he won't make a space ship to get to the moon, and they are gonna knock on your door the very first thing and say, 'We have taken a giant leap for mankind and now we would like to know how to be happy.' They are gonna bother you, wherever you go they are gonna bother you." Then God said, "How about at the bottom of the ocean?" The wise man said, "Forget it, they have submarines so within 2000 years they are gonna come to the bottom of the ocean, they are gonna find you living there and they are gonna have the same eternal question, 'How can I be happy?'" and God said, "I got it, I got it!" And he did not even tell the wise man. But since I am a meditator I know. He decided to hide in the hearts of men because he knew that no one would look inside of themselves for the answer.

"When two egotists meet, it's an I for an I." Vibhavan

So God is hiding inside of each and every one of us, this is where your real freedom is. You are the only master of your being. Of course God would never go to outer space or into your heart without saying goodbye, and he was very attached to Adam and Eve as you know. As he was about to leave planet earth, or at the least the places we look for him, he called Adam and Eve together and said, "I am really happy with you two and I am happy with my creation. It took me six days and I have never done such good work before, so I took a day off and now I am quite bored. I wanna move on and start again. See what I can do the next time, see if I can make some improvements. But for sure I would not leave without giving you each a miracle, each a present. Adam was very, very excited. First of all he was very happy that God was leaving because he was enjoying Eve so much, doing this thing called fucking, that he wanted to be alone with her. He was actually just as finished with God as God was finished with him. He wanted to experience tantra. But he was excited like a little boy, a present, this is fun! From God, what could it be? Must be fucking great! And God said, "Who would like the first miracle?" And Adam could not contain himself and he jumped up and he said, "Me!" So God said, "The miracle, the gift that I am bestowing on you, my Adam, is the ability to pee standing up." And Eve was stuck with the miracle called multiple orgasms.

You know it's difficult to tell a joke in a book because obviously we kids in America, we have heard it all. Very rarely will you read a joke in this book that you haven't heard before. So sometimes I pick these jokes that I feel indicate Zen, I call them Zen koans. It just feels like we have heard all these jokes, but I am hoping that this book goes back to my friends in Europe where I have enjoyed living all these summers of my life. I spend the winters in India each year, and India is just so psychologically far

"Be yourself. Who else is better qualified?" Frank J. Giblin II

away from America that very few Americans journey so far in and so far away from being in and outside of themselves in America. But these jokes that I was talking about, these jokes that you have heard and that you have enjoyed and that you would love to tell me a better joke, these jokes did not make it necessarily to Europe. I don't know why, but every culture is different and certainly they never made it to India where there just don't seem to be even that many Indian jokes to tell. Anyway, I am hoping this book travels and that these jokes will bring a sense of relief because my European friends and my Indian friends love a good joke. Sometimes I throw a little something into the joke that is a little extra from that original joke that you heard, and when you do meet me, if you have a good joke I'd love to hear it. Or send me an e-mail to; krishnaprem@geeyouareyou.com

I would love to get your jokes.

I remember that on one occasion, Brian was visiting me at Geetam and I introduced him to a female guest who was falling in love with Osho. I had a feeling that she was falling for Osho to hide something from her past. She confided in me that she was abused by her grandfather when she was in her first teenage year. Now she was forty-three. I asked Brian to work with her through hypnosis. He pointed out that she was abused once thirty years ago, and since that moment in time, she has abused herself every day for the last thirty years. Brian said simply that she could not change the fact that she was abused, but she could change her emotional involvement with the event. In just one hour of hypnosis plus countless hours of Dynamic Meditation, my friend became more at ease with her life. She lost emotional weight as well as physical weight and was able to begin a healthy relationship for the first time in her life. You might say she lived her teenager years while in a forty-plus body. It's never too late to grow up and enjoy

"You're born an original, don't die a copy." John Mason

your life. George Bernard Shaw said it best, "We don't stop playing because we grow old. We grow old because we stop playing."

Say Your Own Name Meditation by Dr. Brian Alman

Start by focusing on your breathing, inhale and exhale, maybe notice the turning points – just simply focusing, inhale and then exhale.

After a few breaths, as you exhale say your own name to yourself, but not out loud, just say your own name. First name, last name, full name, nickname – whatever favorite name you use when you talk to yourself. Just inhale and on the exhale say your name to yourself, and continue doing this for ten to fifteen breaths. Stay with it, repeating your own name to yourself as you exhale. If you get distracted, because most people do, just keep coming back to your name and saying it on the exhale.

I learned this simple technique from a remarkable woman I met when I was on a teaching tour in India at the OSHO International Meditation Resort. She had gone from being a humble house cleaner to becoming one of the most sought-after healers in all of India. And when I asked if she would share with me the secret of her power, she told me how to "Say Your Own Name." It was her gift to me, and now I'm giving it to you.

When you feel beside yourself, caught up in stress and unhappiness, give this wonderful healer's technique some time and energy, and watch what happens. You'll feel more centered and sure of yourself, more connected with your true, authentic self.

142

But you don't have to wait for a moment of challenge; you'll want to practice this whenever you have the chance. Maybe when you sit down to breakfast; just take a few moments, close your eyes, focus on your breathing and then inhale and say your own name on the exhale. This will just get better and better for you. This is a gold medal winner.

Now, add a whole other dimension to your name, your success, your evolution, your freedom, your self-acceptance and your enLIGHTenment! As you inhale, please say your own goal to yourself (not out loud and this may be easiest to learn with your eyes closed). Most importantly, remember to make this ridiculously easy because that will empower you to be present and relaxed.

For the next 1, 2, 10 or any number of breaths that you choose – remember, ridiculously easy – inhale and say your goal to yourself and then exhale and say your own name to yourself. Eyes open or closed; it's 100% up to you.

If you like, inhale and say to yourself, "I love" and then exhale and say your name.
Your breathing is the bridge.
You are the bridge.
Every cell in your being appreciates your breathing and utilizes it for health, (inner) communication, transmission of ideas and sensations, freedom and Life!

Your breathing is the bridge between your innermost self (your heart and soul) and your outermost self (your body).

STEP ONE: Accept your breathing as it is (eyes open or closed)

life, and the next world." Osho

STEP TWO: Say your own name to yourself on your exhales only (1 or more breaths)

STEP THREE: Say your goal to yourself on the inhales and that can be anything you want – feel free to change this as situations arise and your true, personal needs evolve.

WITH LOVE!

Dr. Brian Alman

www.TruSage.com

"Your personality should not be confused with reality." Krishna Prem

Chapter 6

Tantra: The Supreme Understanding

"Awareness cannot exist with duality, and mind cannot exist without duality. Awareness is non-dual, and mind is dual. So just watch. I don't teach you any solutions. I teach you the solution: Just get back a little and watch. Create a distance between you and your mind."

Beyond Psychology, Osho

Aside from what the parents think, we also have to deal with what others around us think, in other words our social standing or reputation. This is how our friends, college mates, work colleagues, neighbors or the world at large see us. I call it going to the social opinion polls. While some of us pride ourselves in having a good reputation, some of us get off on having a bad reputation. But whether we're popular or unpopular, famous or infamous, respected or disrespected, it only matters if we care what others think. And why do we care what others think? Because we have been trained to see ourselves according to others, trained to compare and measure ourselves by others and to listen to others rather than ourselves. At grass roots level, we have been trained to believe there is an "other" in the first place.

We have also been trained to inform others of our place in the world. We add letters before our names to let people know our social standing, marital status and gender, whether we are a Lord, a Knight or a Sir, a Mr. or if we are a woman, a Queen, a Dame, or a Miss. Then we add letters after our names, to let people know how educated we are, whether we are BA, MBA or PhD, an FCA or a

"I am free of all prejudices. I hate everyone equally." W. C. Fields

CEO. And while some of us love the formal, grandiose titles, others of us are just as happy being known as "a nice guy," "a cute girl" or "a crazy dude." I guess we all get off on different definitions, just as we all like different flavors of ice cream.

But at the end of the day, are you your social status and reputation? Are you other people's opinions, judgments and expectations? I notice we have this big thing about judgments, judging and being judgmental. But really, what's the big deal? Basically, a judgment is a thought, and judging is all the mind knows how to do. In fact, it's what it does best.

Every single thought we have is a judgment of some kind; "the grass is greener," "that dog is mangy," "this pizza is crap," or "that woman is a total bitch!" So what? Judgments are words, words are thoughts. Words and thoughts are like clouds floating in the sky; they come and go and they are not you. Just look at the newspapers – movie stars, pop stars and political stars are all the rage today and on the trash heap tomorrow. Are you what others think Think again!

I'll never forget the first time I heard Joni Mitchell sing the refrain, "I've seen clouds from both sides now." For me Joni was looking at her emotional love life from every vantage point, the good, the bad and ugly. Joni became the witness, watching her life as an empty sky, looking at her clouds from both sides now without confusing who she is with her emotions. This is what I understand to be an emotionally intelligent person....

My male version of an emotional-intelligence flunking grade was with the U.S. Army, which left me completely identified with my emotions.

146

"A meditative man has insight. He can see how he himself created his problems.

I thought all that guilt, shame, sadness, disappointment and self-hate was me. But after years of meditating, you know what I found out? That my feelings weren't me. You see, who you are precedes your feelings. Feelings only exist because U do. You were there first. It's like you're the sky, and your emotions are clouds floating along in it. Some clouds are white and fluffy, some are menacing and grey and some shed rain, but they all naturally appear and disappear. Emotions are the same; they arise from thoughts, hang out in the body for a while, then as fast as they come, they go. That's what they do. So whenever misery is knocking on your door, don't try and lock it out or push it away, just open the door and let it in. It can't stay forever – emotions are always in motion, they are not permanent. Besides, misery gives life meaning... misery is God appearing as an asshole!

See, the goal of life isn't to be devoid of emotions, isn't to be even-keeled one hundred percent of the time. No, that's for robots. It's to allow the emotions to flow, and to know who you are beyond them. I have plenty of emotions swilling around in my tub, only I know they're not me. So next time you're thinking, "God, I'm so angry," "God, I'm so depressed!" or even "God, I'm so happy!" check out, is that me? How do you label yourself? Temperamental or even-tempered? Emotional, moody or volatile? Open, vulnerable and sensitive? Or closed, hard and insensitive? Watch what feelings you try to hang onto and the ones you like to push away and ask, are they me? The truth is your fabulous thoughts, your beautiful moods and your sensuous body will come and go, but the big U always remains.

One analogy Osho referred to is that there is only one sky to fly in. To me this meant that once I am in the sky looking at both sides of my clouds now, not only would I not be so indentified with my clouds, but I could also look down and see human beings polishing

147

And then, naturally he stops creating them." Osho

their own separate windows down on the earth. That every human being who is not in the sky for their own reasons thinks that he or she is separate from the whole and acting independently of everyone else. Yes there is only one sky, and seven billion people on planet earth are seeing the world through seven billion individual rose-colored windows. And you ask how seven billion people can be wrong about a Buddha or a Christ? Don't ask, realize....

It's true to say that Geetam was becoming more famous, and being just two hours east of LA it was also attractive to the Hollywood community. Emmy award-winning actor Peter Coyote, who went on to star in Roman Polanski's "Bitter Moon," frequented Geetam because he loved Osho's active meditations. It must be a requirement that all great method actors are able to scream at the top of their lungs whether they mean it or not, and I for one was impressed at Peter's let-go. I wasn't surprised when one day I got a call from Peter's good friend, director Mark Rydell, asking me if I could coach Bette Midler for his film "The Rose." It was my job to convince the audience that Midler was in fact about to go mad, and it was one of the easiest jobs I ever had. Not only is Bette Midler talented, she's also very lively. My audition for this job as Bette Midler's madness-mentor was to do the Dynamic meditation live and uncensored on the lawn at the home of the actor James Coburn, with Peter giving a running commentary to James Coburn and Mark Rydell on the method of my madness. I gave a command performance and was duly given the opportunity to share my insanity with Bette Midler on set. If I remember correctly, Bette was nominated for an academy award. James Coburn and I became good friends and when Osho was asking if he could stay in America, one thousand pop psychologists gladly responded to this invitation and wrote letters of recommendation

148

on Osho's behalf. At the top of the pile was the letter from James Coburn suggesting that America would benefit from such a creative presence as Osho.

Also staying at the home of James Coburn was none other than the Karmapa Lama, who was the lama that I first went to India to meet when I bumped into Osho by accident. I was very excited at the chance of having a private audience with the Karmapa; even though I was already in love I am not a fool. After sitting in silence with the Karmapa, he asked me where I live. I remember laughing to myself that I live in Osho-consciousness, but I was still just an old-fashioned American boy at the time and I gave him driving instructions how to get to the Geetam Rajneesh Sannyas Ashram. I know this sounds funny but the Karmapa, like Osho, loved to keep his pedal to the metal, in other words, he loved a fast car. In James Coburn's garage was a red Ferrari and the Karmapa loved the rush of taking the curves around the Hollywood Hills as if he was driving on a freeway. You take a master out of India and the first thing they get is a speeding ticket! In fact as the story goes, one time Osho was stopped for driving over the speed limit while he was in Oregon and he said to the police officer, "That's impossible, because I have a speed-breaker on my speedometer." His Rolls Royce was incapable of speeding, and he asked the officer to actually time him one more time because he was going to have his lawyer write to Rolls Royce. Osho got a speeding ticket to no one's surprise and I don't know if he ever heard back from the Rolls Royce people. Osho was indeed lucky he didn't get two speeding tickets. He was also lucky never to crash and burn, even though it is rumored he ran off the road here and there. It appears he was attracted to soft-shoulders. The Karmapa was the same way when he came to speedy America.

The Karmapa kept pulling on my beard and I found out later that in his past life the Karmapa Lama had a beard similar to mine, similarly as alive as mine. When his life was threatened by an outlaw band of insincere meditators, the story goes that his beard was woven into the tail of a horse and when the horse was whipped and took off, taking the beard with it, so the Karmapa saved his life by letting go of his beard. In this lifetime he was clean-shaven. Please don't get this confused with the truth; it's just a wonderful story.

Speaking about stories, Osho many years later in discourse spoke about how when the master asks you where you live, he is not talking about your physical address but that home is where the heart is. By now the Karmapa Lama had left his body and again I learned to laugh at my own unconsciousness. I just said a silent prayer to myself that I hope the Karmapa Lama grows a beautiful beard in his next lifetime. Besides laughing at myself, I acknowledge the beauty of not being corrected. Masters seem to have infinite patience and trust that one day the unconscious being sitting in front of him, will grow up. Masters always live in a state of timeless time.

My body turned sixty-five years old. In America that means you can retire so I went to the Social Security Office to find out if I had any benefits for health insurance, because I was sure that since I left America at age twenty-nine, I never worked enough to actually receive Social Security. There I was sitting with a very attractive, well-dressed woman who was clearly in a very good mood. I said, "I'm surprised to see a government employee looking so happy." And she said, "I'm in a very good mood because I'm about to take early retirement at age sixty-two." I said to her, "That's probably why I've been happy since I was twenty-nine." We both laughed

"Everything in life need not be explained. We have no responsibility to explain

and she said, "Well let me see who you are." I said, "My name is Michael Allen Mogul." and she said, "I'm sorry you don't exist." Being a man of Zen, I picked up my right foot and lightly stepped on her left toe, and out of shock she said, "Ouch!" and I said, "Excuse me I thought you said I didn't exist." I said to her very simply, "Being the kind of guy I am, I actually felt that this was a compliment that I don't exist!" It's the kind of compliment that massages my spiritual ego. I remember Osho getting attention when he said to me that the difficulty with my young Jewish friends is that they are so ready to trade in their bank balance for a spiritual bank account. It's great to give up your bank account if that's what you want, but it doesn't pave the way to god-realization, a good beginning can lead anywhere, of course, and donations are always appreciated.

I told her I remembered my Social Security number, but I'm not so sure I haven't told the same lie about this number as I have about my name, so that eventually it became the truth; so let's try this number on for size, 01732****. She looked up at me in shock, and without giving anything away, she hinted, almost because she doesn't know how to lie, that this could, in fact, be me. I said, "Tell me my name," and she immediately sat up straight and said, "I'm sorry but that's against the law to tell you your name," and we both smiled, but her smile was more serious than mine in that moment. I said to her, "Please tell me my initials," and without hesitation she said. "KP," I said, "Are you shitting me?" She said, "Can we please keep this professional?" I said, "Forgive me but you just reminded me of all my four sisters at once!" I said, "Tell me just one thing, this gentleman in question, is his name Krishna Prem?" She said, "My god, how did you know that?" The memories rushed my mind....

anything to anybody." Osho

It's now over thirty years ago since I bought Geetam Ashram in Lucerne Valley, California in order for it to become a non-profit organization. It dawned on me that Michael Mogul didn't sound as religious as Swami Krishna Prem, male seeker of truth. Before 9/11 you could change your name every day because your real name was your Social Security number. After 9/11 you need to be as straight as that nine-digit number, after 9/11 the name better be the same as your number or you're not eligible for Medicare. Funnily enough, by now this woman and I were flirting with each other, just totally enjoying the fact that I exist, and I simply have a soft spot for anybody that won't be at work tomorrow morning, and then she said to me, "The difference between you being a derelict, which means no Social Security and no Medicare, is one day of work in one quarter." I needed to make 1,050 dollars and if I did this, I would be entitled to not only insurance but a grand total of 323 dollars a month, she said, "Are you capable of work?" I said, "I'm full of rust but I'm going to crash though my resistance and participate in the world for as long as it takes for me to make a grand."

Needless to say I was able to pull off a miracle and make 1,050 dollars in one month by promising my older brother Max that I am renouncing meditation, that I have completely mended my wicked ways, and having seen the light, capitalism is now my god. I said I'll need 1,050 dollars a month as a start-up salary. He paid me in advance and I quit a month later without giving notice and retired to live happily ever after for a second time, with Social Security benefits intact.

I was once sitting in front of Osho and a young man mentioned to him, "You know, my family isn't having a really good time with the concept of me being a sannyasin." And Osho said, "Well, that's only ordinary that parents wouldn't be excited that you have

152

"Your task is not to seek for love, but merely to seek and find all the barriers

chosen this life." And Osho chuckled as if to say that if your parents ever knew they were creating a sannyasin, your father would have got the best blowjob of his entire life. I don't think parents are ever happy with their children because everybody is an individual. Deep down beyond your conditioning, beyond your family, you are just visiting that family. In a sense the best you can show is gratitude to a stranger for being there for you. I am not presenting this as the truth, I am just saying what I have observed that your mother and you have just as much in common as any other two people in the world. And I often think and meditate on that statement "blood is thicker than water," and the answer is that there is no difference in the thickness except in the mind. I say that I am as attached to my family as you are to yours. It's just that once in a while I remember to take a moment and see everyone as not two instead of everyone is my family.

Another time I was sitting with Osho and just trying to remember what I had memorized. It was the second or third time I was sitting with him alone and I wanted to say something really, really brilliant like, "While I was meditating I had a satori." Or, "I am enlightened now ever since I met you." I wanted to say something that would make me feel worthy in his eyes. And as I looked into his eyes, all these great thoughts about satori and enlightenment and instant coffee just disappeared and he asked me how I was feeling? And I said, "I feel lucky." And he just began to laugh and at the time Vivek was his personal caretaker, and he just looked at her and laughed and he looked back at me and he said, "You know it's so great everybody comes to me and wants to talk about satori and wants to talk about enlightenment and I am so happy to hear that finally someone just feels lucky." And he said, "I will tell you what, you stay here with me until you don't feel

within yourself that you have built against it." Rumi

lucky, until you feel enlightened, until you have had a satori. You just stay right here with me as long as you have lucky feeling." It was like a hex if you think about it, that's thirty-eight years ago he said that to me, and I continue to feel lucky, I continue not to have satoris, I continue not to be enlightened but I still have that little twinkle in my eye, that little dance in my step which maybe you might remember as being in love with someone. Osho spoke to me about writing a little song about the moments when I feel lucky and he said, "You know you don't always feel good, life can suck sometimes and once in a while you bump into a happy, lucky moment." He said, "I want you to write a song about these moments, maybe they are years apart, maybe one moment is followed by another moment in that very same day, but basically just write a little song about the good times and then sing it to yourself during the bad times." And he said that one reason he has asked me to do that is because bliss, ecstasy, when you are really thrilled with life, it takes absolutely no time. No time is taken up. Just think about it, the last time you were really happy, how long did it last? You probably don't have a good answer but if I said to you how long you were miserable the last time your girlfriend left you, you probably can tell me to the minute. "It was three months, eleven days and four minutes I was just absolutely miserable." And that's how we are, we remember the bad times. The bad times take up time; the good times take up no time at all. It's one of the mysteries of life.

Just take a moment, forget about this book, write a little song about the happy moments and sing it to yourself. Don't waste your time by writing a book about your lousy moments; it would be bigger than the Bible. That book, your tragedy would be bigger than the Bible. So write a very short song, "I Want to Hold Your Hand" by the Beatles would be a great example. Just a few words

154

"If you want to know who you are, you will have to forget the whole world.

that represent that good moment; tie together a great moment when you were seven, a great moment when you were thirteen, and just put all those moments together, write a little song and sing it to yourself. It may not become a number one hit for anybody but you, but I guarantee it will bring a little smile to your face.

We all know it does not take a master to help us see into life's mysteries. I will never forget I was playing tennis with a friend of mine named Milarepa, and he is the kind of guy that the girls really liked and he liked them. My god he had a really good life and I am a working man, I never had it so easy and I was totally jealous at the girl I was dating then, because she was interested in me and she was interested in somebody else and for all I knew she would have given both of us up for Milarepa. Anyway I said to Mila, "You know, I am really fucking jealous right now." I said, "Do you ever get jealous?" He looked at me and he said, "I no longer get jealous. Jealous does not happen for me." And it was like the tennis ball hit me right between the eyes. All of my jealousy simply fell away. I was not jealous. I don't know how that works; we have all had that moment with a great teacher or a great coach. All of a sudden the mind just drops, the heart just drops. You are just here and now; I no longer was jealous. I can remember again the racket was swinging much more than it was swinging when I was thinking about jealousy. There was a let-go in my arm because my heart was beginning to relax. And when I saw my girlfriend later on and I did not come from the space called jealousy, my god she was very, very attracted to me. She really thought I was great, she couldn't understand the freedom I was allowing her, just the space I was in and the space she could join me in and we actually got together except that later on she was the one that got jealous. So just know that this space called beyond jealous, see if you can go there the next time you are jealous. Don't try, it will kill you to try,

155

but see if it exists for you, see if you can be bigger than your emotions, see if you can allow space.

Another thing that happened for me when I was living at Geetam; I was very, very, very, very much in love with a girl named Anubodhi. She was great; it was like everything you could want. I know you have been there, even if only in your mind at least you have been there. Anyway I was totally in love with this girl and we were taking a walk in the desert, it was a beautiful starry night and then the moon came out and the stars disappeared. This is the desert and so the full moon was really, really big and really, really full. And you could literally see the man in the moon just enjoying himself, relaxing, letting the light in, and she said to me, "Doesn't the moon look like a big piece of watermelon?" To be honest it did not look like a big piece of watermelon but I was so in love with her that it was poetry in motion. Anyway a few weeks later, it must have been a month because now the moon is full again and there is a young man, his name is Geetananda. He came to see me and we were taking a walk in the night and checking out the stars and then the moon rose and the moon was full and he looked at me and he said, "My god, doesn't the moon look like a big piece of watermelon?" Well, I nearly died because we had been discussing the whole night whether it was right for him to live at Geetam, and in my heart of hearts I knew it was right for him to live there but I knew that my relationship was over. I knew that when these two pieces of watermelon met it was gonna be a very wet situation. I went directly into the pits and I am here to tell you it took him about three or four days to meet her and it was over for me and I will never forget it, it was a terrible, terrible time in my life, but I knew that he was a valuable man in the community and I knew she was a valuable woman in the community. I knew I had to say yes because the community was

156

"Meditation means the art of being alone. And love means the art of being

my life. You know there is a Buddhist expression "To be at the feet of the awakened one, to be at to the commune of the awakened one, to be at the truth of the awakened one." So I did not really have a choice, I said yes. They met, shit! I hate it even to this day; even though this story is twenty-five years old I can remember it because I hated it. It was not one of the happy moments in my song.

Maybe this next example is totally different but in one moment in time, I was simply unhappy living in the OSHO International Meditation Resort in Pune, India. I was basically feeling flat. And it's really funny when you live in a meditation surrounding and you are in a really good mood and your energy is light, often times you walk towards a door and the door opens, a friend just opens the door for you. You could have done it yourself, you feel so light, the door feels so light, everything is light. When the light is on the door is open. And if you are in a shit mood and you are a drag and you are feeling really heavy and you walk towards the same door and you think that door is going to be opened, there is a really good chance you are going to just smack your face on a very solid glass door. You may have had that happen to you. Anyway, I was in a really bad space and it went on for a while. One day I walked outside my room in Osho House and there was a guy crawling around on the floor with his ass towards my face and I said, "Hey, what are you up to?" thinking maybe the guy was up to no good. And the guy stood up and he ran his hands through his hair and straightened his glasses and it turned out to be my next door neighbor Jayesh who kind of is the... you might have heard Osho saying, "I leave you my dream." Anyway he straightened out his glasses and he ran his hands through his hair and it's simply that he had dropped his keys on the ground. And we just had a chance to laugh together because it was a fresh moment. I said, "Hey Jayesh,

with people, the art of being together." Radkhi

now that I have your attention, I just wanna let you know that while I was in a really down space and in a bad mood I did not feel any juice coming your way toward me, and I just wanna let you know maybe a simple hello in that moment might have helped me out." And he was really cute and he said, "It's not my job. I did ask after you, I saw you weren't in a very good space but I just did not have a chance to pump you up. I had more on my mind than that." He said, "But to be honest, you look great right now. What did you do for yourself?" And I said, "You know I stopped flirting with women and I started flirting with myself. And I went on a little diet just for myself and I combed my hair just for myself and I did a lot of selfish things just for myself." What I am really trying to say right now is often times we try and get out of a bad space in ourselves by trying to be attractive to somebody else, hoping that person will smile and bring us out. And it's time not to leave it up to somebody else for us to be in a good space. The other thing I am trying to say right now, which is really not such an easy concept to get because we don't have very much training in the West, is to actually be selfish. To take our energy back and start pumping ourselves up from the inside out. Not from the outside in but actually from the inside out. By going back into who we are, seeing what it is that is making us so uncomfortable and so unloving right now.

Meditation is very simple. It's the art of being alone. Meditation actually comes first and love follows, at least this is how I see it in terms of awareness. Consciousness is not a "we." There is no such thing as collective consciousness. In fact when Buddha and Mahavira met, in the golden days of enlightenment, while their disciples argued about who is the higher and most enlightened master in the world, Mahavira and Buddha simply walked past each other because there was nothing to say. What does this mean

"Awareness cannot exist with duality, and mind cannot exist without duality.

in terms of relationship? I don't know, we have to look at it together, but basically what I am saying is if you are feeling good you are gonna meet good feelings. But it's not a collective thing. So please next time you are down and out don't go through that old address book looking for somebody that could make you happy. Sit on that book, forget about that book and sing yourself a happy song, move around, move that energy, don't sit on your fucking ass and feel miserable for yourself. At least move your ass, wriggle a little, shoot some baskets.

In my distant past, I was giving bodywork sessions in Los Angeles area. I would always suggest to my clients who wanted to meet a juicy partner to actually act alive and juicy, not down and out. In other words, you attract how you act. Here is a moment with Osho that can change your life from this moment on. How do I know? Because it changed my life;

"Choose happiness – that means you are choosing the effect – and then see what happens. Choose ecstasy and see what happens. Choose to be blissful and see what happens. Your whole life will change immediately and you will see miracles happening around you – because now you have created the effect and causes will have to follow. This will look magical; you can even call it the law of magic. The first is the law of science and the second is the law of magic. Religion is magic, and you can be the magician. That's what I teach you: to be the magician, to know the secret of magic."

Try it! You have been trying the other your whole life – not only this but many other lives also. Now listen to me! Try this magic formula, this mantra I give to you. Create the effect and see what happens; causes immediately surround you, they follow. Don't wait for the causes; you have waited long enough. Choose happiness and you will be happy.

Awareness is non-dual, and mind is dual." Osho

Another time I was sitting with Osho and I had just come from California, from Geetam, and he said to the boy in front of me, "And how long did you come for?" The boy wanted to impress Osho with his dedication, so he closed his eyes and opened his eyes and said, "Osho, I am here forever." And Osho closed his eyes and opened his eyes and he said, "Can you come for longer the next time?" I wished I could have stayed forever but I was running Geetam and could stay for only three months a year at the most. So sometimes saying that I love you or I am here for forever is absolutely not the right thing to say and to be true to yourself, is to be true to the other person. There is no difference. So the next time you are feeling really completely jealous, it is a sign of life. Watch the mind with all its problems; just watch. Mind is actually your only problem. All other problems, jealousy for example, are just ideas of the mind. Basically it does not matter if you are fucked; it does not matter if you are free. It matters only that you know where you are coming from right now.

Joseph Campbell, the great American mystic once said, "The world is perfect, it's a perfect mess."

All I am saying is let's let life happen, let's not make plans. John Lennon said, "Life is what happens to you while you're making other plans." Let's not get married, let's not get divorced, let's be aware what is life saying to us right now, and when we come to that answer that we are light, the question simply disappears. There is no answer but there is a situation when the question dissolves and we are just in what is best known throughout the world of meditation as the here and now.

Ah, religion – touchy as it is, we must touch on it! I was born into a Jewish family, raised by Jewish people in the Jewish religion, but I am not Jewish! Because I wasn't very good at

"Acceptance is a magic key. Accept yourself as you are! And in that acceptance,

school, I had to spend a lot of time after school learning what most kids learned in school. So while most smart Jewish kids went to Hebrew lessons after regular school, I didn't go because of my learning disabilities. So at the tender age of thirteen, at my Bar Mitzvah, which is the time when a Jewish boy becomes a man, I had had no religious training at all. However that didn't save me, because Judaism, in a sense, is not a religion, it's a way of life. So, even though I didn't know shit about the Torah, at that point in my life, I already was Jewish from beginning to end anyway.

Besides, I do love the jokes!

A man walking along Broadway was confronted by a business girl whispering, "Love for sale."

The man said, "Sure, if you could do it the Jewish way."

The girl said, "If you teach me to do it the Jewish way, I will give it to you for half price."

The man replied, "That is the Jewish way."

A Jewish couple was honeymooning at Niagara Falls. The boy's money ran out after a week, but he and his bride were having such a good time they wanted to stay longer. So he wired his father for more money. His telegram read: "Dear Dad. It's great here. Want to stay longer. Please send money. Love, Son." The father wired back: "Dear Son. It's great everywhere. Come home. Love, Dad."

But joking aside, is this who we are? The special beliefs we hold, the special clothes we wear, the special foods we eat, the special rituals we follow and the special holidays we celebrate? Aren't these just things we believe, say and do? I mean, are we really born a certain religion? Look at your new-born son, does he

intelligence arises." Osho

have a religion? Did he come out of the womb a Christian, a Baptist, a Methodist, a Sikh or a Hindu? Or did you tell him what religion he was? You know, poor kid, he might not even know he's a little boy yet, let alone a Zoroastrian. Maybe the only thing he knows is he's alive and that he's here right now. Maybe right now he's just being himself. But I wonder, in twenty years time, what religious beliefs he'll have and who he'll think he is?

We aren't born into a certain religion, we're raised in a certain religious climate, around people holding certain religious beliefs, and more often than not we adopt those same beliefs and way of life as our own. But just because we're born of parents who believe in Christ, doesn't make us a Christian. I mean, strictly speaking, wasn't Jesus the first and last Christian? And some of you may be wincing by now, because like I say, it is a touchy subject. Some people are extremely identified with their religious beliefs while others not so much so. Most people I know are only part-time religious. Basically, they go to church Sunday morning and for one hour, they're these terrifically devoted people who love, cherish, pray and sing, then they go home and for the remaining 167 hours in the week, they just carry on with their ordinary lives. So, the big G for them is more like a habit, an insurance policy or a social activity, someone to pray to when the going gets rough or someone to keep at arm's length when they've gone astray. And they're believing and worshipping and praying to God, but they don't really know who God is and they're not really seeing that truth is right under their nose.

God to Jesus: "Just what the hell did you tell those people?"

So I hereby announce a new religion which will blossom over the next five hundred years. Devotees call it The Innernet. Here

162

"Life is not something to be thought about, it is something to be danced, to be

are the first two commandments from The Innernet, formerly known as www.com:

A water bearer in China had two large pots, each hung on the ends of a pole, which he carried across his neck. One of the pots had a crack in it, while the other pot was perfect and always delivered a full portion of water. At the end of the long walk from the stream to the house, the cracked pot arrived only half full.

For a full two years this went on daily, with the bearer delivering only one and a half pots full of water to his house. Of course, the perfect pot was proud of its accomplishments, perfect for which it was made. But the poor cracked pot was ashamed of its own imperfection, and miserable that it was able to accomplish only half of what it had been made to do.

After two years of what it perceived to be a bitter failure, it spoke to the water bearer one day by the stream. "I am ashamed of myself, and because this crack in my side causes water to leak out all the way back to your house."

The bearer said to the pot, "Did you notice that there were flowers only on your side of the path, but not on the other pot's side? That's because I have always known about your flaw, and I planted flower seeds on your side of the path, and every day while we walk back, you've watered them. For two years I have been able to pick these beautiful flowers to decorate the table. Without you being just the way you are, there would not be this beauty to grace the house."

And there's one more Innernet story I really like that goes like this:

loved, to be celebrated." Osho

An old Red Indian is teaching his grandson about life: "A fight is going on inside me," he said to the boy.

"It is a terrible fight and it is between two wolves, one is evil – he is anger, envy, sorrow, regret, greed, arrogance, self-pity, guilt, resentment, inferiority, lies, false-pride, superiority, and ego. The other is good – he is joy, peace, love, hope, serenity, humility, kindness, benevolence, empathy, generosity, truth, compassion and faith.

"This same fight is going on inside you – and inside every other person, too."

The grandson thought about it for a minute and then asked his grandfather, "Which wolf will win?"

The old Indian simply replied, "The one you feed."

Alternatively, we may pride ourselves in being beyond all that religious stuff and all those illusions about god. No, now we're a fully paid-up member of the spiritual path. We're a full-time seeker, an official disciple, an A-List devotee, or the renunciate to end all renunciates. And now we're calling ourselves absolute oneness, infinite love or eternal consciousness itself. But again, we need to stop and ask ourselves, isn't this just another form of identity? And no, I'm not banging on about searching, not banging on about the path at all. Seeking and meditating are definitely a great preparation, but calling yourself the greatest meditator on earth is still limiting who you are.

"Never take life seriously. Nobody gets out alive anyway."

Why do our passport photos always look so awful? Why is it that the only photo we're destined to carry around for the next ten years or so doesn't really do us justice? Is it some cruel joke of existence or just a great opportunity to laugh at ourselves? Time to look at nationality and ask how identified you are with the country you were born in? How patriotic are you? How many national flags do you have flying outside your house? How elated do you feel when "your country" wins another Olympic gold medal? How miffed do you feel when they lose the World Cup? I mean, it's only a game, isn't it?

I notice that Russians often say, "In my country this, in my country that," while Americans always say "We did this, and we did that." "We're sending aid to Cambodia," "We're sending troops to Afghanistan," "We're fighting the forces of evil," "We're 100 billion in debt." But who is this famous "We?" You and a few of your friends kicking around? Or you and all the other guys living on that whole chunk of land between Canada and Mexico, colored in pastel pink on the map? Or maybe you're more identified with a particular ethnic group, tribe or race? Or your favorite football team; The Dallas Cowboys, The Houston Oilers or the Miami Dolphins? And how often do you say, "We're playing the San Diego Chargers next week," or "We kicked their ass last week." Just because you've bought the T-shirt, the scarf and the cap, is that who you are?

I bought a T-shirt on Maui at Casanova's, the restaurant, which nails our conditioning;

Heaven is where the police are British,

the chefs Italian,

the mechanics German,

"The universe is within you." Nisagardatta

the lovers French,

and it's all organized by the Swiss.

Hell is where the police are German,

the chefs are British,

the mechanics French,

the lovers Swiss,

and it's all organized by the Italians.

And it's not about right and wrong or better and worse, it's simply that we all grow up in different countries and learn to do things differently. For sure, if I'd grown up in Tahiti, the Congo or Outer Mongolia, I would naturally be movin' and groovin' differently, speaking a different language and following a different cultural code. But is this who we are – the country we were born in and the cultural conditioning we received? Are any of us American, English, African, Australian, Chinese... or Polish for that matter?

How did I find out that I was Polish? I told my mother a Polish joke, which I thought was very funny:
"What does a Polish girl do with her vibrator? She chips her teeth."
It was one of the first dirty jokes I ever told my mother, only when she didn't laugh and I asked her why, she said it was because she was Polish. It then took me three days to figure out that if she was Polish, then so was I. Most of us love to generalize about people of different nationalities, and pigeon-hole them, and of course, laugh about them too;

"The eternal lover is within you. Once you have found it, you are absolutely

An American, an Englishman and a Frenchman are on a boat. After a while the boat begins to sink, and the Englishman, being a gentleman, says, "Women and children first!"

The American says, "Fuck them!"

The Frenchman says, "Do we have time?"

An Englishman goes to visit his doctor. "Doc," he says, "I'm madly in love with this Polish girl. You've got to help me become a Polack."

"Are you sure?" says the doctor. "In order to do that, we've got to surgically remove half your brain."

The man then tells him that it doesn't matter what it takes, he wants the operation anyway. Afterwards, when the man wakes up, he finds the doctor standing beside his bed.

"I'm terribly sorry," says the doctor, "We made a terrible mistake. We removed three-quarters of your brain."

The man slaps his forehead and cries, "Ah, mama mia!"

Nationality is a joke! Some people get mightily offended if you joke about their nationality or their country, but that's only because they think it's them. You know, really when we strip off our cultural wrapping paper, we're all the same underneath. I think this story I received in an e-mail sums it up nicely:

Stepping over the border into an unknown country, a traveller saw an old man sitting under a tree. He approached him and asked him about the people in this new land he had just entered.

The old man answered by asking, "How are the people in your country?"

167

content with yourself." Osho

"Oh," said the traveller, "They are friendly, hospitable and cheerful."

"Well," the old man said, "You'll find them to be the same in my country too."

A few days later another traveller arrived and approached the man under the tree by asking him about the people in this new land he had just entered.

The old man responded by asking, "How are the people in your country?"

"Oh," said the traveller, "They are always in a rush, they have very little time for each other and their main concern in life is how much money they can make."

The old man shrugged and said, "You'll find them to be the same in my country."

We divide the globe into different sections, into East and West, North and South, this continent and that sub-continent, third-world countries and first-class nations. However, if we dissolve the borders between countries, erase the lines on our maps, and remove the labels we have stuck on these slices of land, what nationality are we then? Who are we beneath our colorful flags, our national costumes and our patriotic beliefs, that's what I wanna know.

You know when I first got back to the states in '74 I only had one little Osho book, that same book. I went by the reading library and I bought the book from the bookseller and I still had it crumpled in my pocket. It's the only book I have ever read of Osho and I just put it away and I spent a couple of years in my life picking up jobs here and there, making some money, trying to save

168

enough to get back to India and letting my beard grow, letting my heart open, letting my mind wonder. I didn't read and I did only one meditation, Dynamic. I would watch, and just be, and I screamed a lot. Every once in a while I would just scream. I used to breathe for ten minutes and then I would scream for ten minutes. Then I would carry on with the mantra "hoo," then I would relax. So I would meditate for an hour each day by breathing and letting-go. But I did not read and I was one of the only sannyasins in the whole world at the time, so it's not like I had many people to talk about Osho to. I just let the experience go deeper and deeper into who I am. And I will never forget I was working in West Virginia at the time that I was doing some maintenance work for an environmental company. A very nice little job, I made a lot of money because I was a vegetarian by now and I had an expense account for food because the office was in Boston and I was sent out in the field into the West Virginia area. We were moderating air pollution and I was maintaining the buildings. I don't know why I am no longer a vegetarian necessarily, but at that time it was almost like a religion to be a vegetarian. And there I was and my co-worker said to me, "You know you have to put down in your expense account that you also had a steak. Because if I put down fourteen dollars for a steak and you put down two dollars for mashed potatoes, it makes me look like I'm spending too much money." So just to be a nice guy, I used to put down that I had a steak also. God, I did so well. Expense accounts can be really fun and I had to support my co-workers. I certainly wasn't thinking of myself.

Anyway, this is a past life. We're not talking about right now; we're talking about a thirty-years-young man working in the field. I made quite a bit of money, I did really well plus it was a great job. And then there was a moment when I got laid off because I

J. Krishnamurti

was no longer needed by this company; it had been two years. I was laid off at a time of huge unemployment, but instead of taking the unemployment at that very moment I just got the hell out of West Virginia. And I headed for New York City where I was getting my visa and I was going to India in December when the weather is very beautiful and warm, and I did not wanna carry anything that I wouldn't need. I was dressed in my orange clothes; in my orange sport coat and in my orange jeans and my orange shoes and on the plane from West Virginia to New York I re-read that book that I hadn't read for two years, and all I can say is that the book was alive again in a different way. I had just gone deeper into who I am without having read a word, without having spoken to anyone in particular. Just by being in love and by meditating silently to myself, my whole life was changed. Can I prove it? No. Do I give a shit? No. Do you give a shit? No. But you may wanna prove it to yourself. You may wanna take some time to pick up an Osho book, pick up a book on meditation, go into it, meditate on it, read it again in two years and see how much life has changed. See if I am bullshitting you, or if I'm maybe coming from somewhere. I don't know. It's up to you.

Funny things happen. There I am in the middle of New York City and it is cold. New York is snowing and I am there in an orange cotton sport coat. Orange cotton jeans. I am basically freezing my ass off. My only choice is to keep moving as quickly as possible to get on a plane for India. I was crossing the street to go into the passport office to renew my passport, then on to the Indian embassy to get a new visa. And a bag lady stopped me in the middle at the intersection, as crazy as a three dollar bill. She looked me in the eyes and she said, "You certainly know how to dress for the winter." And I will never forget it because I did feel on fire. I was hot; I was going home. You may have heard this

170

story because a lot of people when they become enlightened don't know who to talk to. And they certainly can't talk to you and me; we are such ordinary human beings. So what they would do is they would go to a mad house. Especially in India many, many enlightened people as soon as they have the experience of becoming enlightened, would go to their local mad house and talk to the in-mates to see if these in-mates could see that they were enlightened. Because many times crazy people are the only people that are in the moment. The problem with crazy people in the moment is they also have consciousness. They don't have any relationship with who they are. So again maybe an enlightened person is just a nut that is present and knows who he is.

Meeting Osho was a happy beginning for me, like meeting an inner lover, and equally an unhappy ending of my relationship with Marcia, now Krishna Priya. My gut told me that my relationship was in trouble and I went to Osho to get to the heart of the matter. I was sure Osho's advice would not only heal my relationship, but also help my friends like you as we finally hear the truth about relating.

I booked a leaving darshan with Osho to say goodbye to him as I was making a complete circle by returning to California to open a commune based on his meditations. Krishna Priya chose to stay behind until my dream came true, then she would join me. Osho agreed with Krishna Priya while I simply wasn't sure which way was up. In front of a burning candle I rehearsed what I was going to ask Osho about my relationship until all that was left of me was a wax wave on my bedroom floor.

I hadn't been apart from my beloved for two years and I was nervous about being without her. I wanted to ask Osho whether I could trust that she'd follow me to California. Could I be sure that

171

doing the impossible." St. Francis of Assisi

she wouldn't fall in love with someone else? I was simply beside myself, and by now I was even jealous of Osho as I was no longer the most important man in my woman's life; I didn't know whether to relation-shit or go blind.

Darshan in 1975 was in Lao Tzu House on the front car porch. Ten of us were scheduled to sit with him one-to-one and I was going to be number ten. It felt like an eternity before it was my turn. Finally Osho looked at the boy in the ninth position and Osho's eyes were so big, they overflowed onto me and I thought he was gesturing me to come forward. Eagerly I got up, but of course it wasn't my turn and he told me to have patience and I promptly sat down again.

I was so embarrassed I could have died. The ninth boy came to sit in front of Osho and as soon as he sat down, he began to cry. And he wouldn't stop crying and Osho waited, and finally Osho broke the silence and said to him, "What seems to be the problem?" And the boy related this story, "I bought a brand new pair of sandals today and when I got out of Kundalini meditation at five-fifteen, my sandals were gone!" And then he burst into tears again.

Osho closed his eyes and when the boy stopped crying, Osho opened his eyes again and he said to the young boy, "I can't help you with your loss, but what I can suggest is that tomorrow you go M. G. Road and you buy another new pair of sandals, and when you go to Kundalini meditation, you take one new sandal off and you put it on the top middle shelf and you take the other new sandal and you put it on the bottom shelf on the far left."

And then he added, "No one ever steals one sandal!"

"Meditation is not a question of conquering or seizing, it is a question of

And then the boy's tears turned into laughter, and it looked to me like Osho was very proud of himself. He was just beaming with the biggest smile you've ever seen in your life. Everyone else was laughing. And then Osho reached out and held the boy's hands, they stood up at the same time and, as if music began playing, Osho did a tiny dance with the boy and then, still beaming, namastéd everyone and walked out, and that was the end of darshan.

I felt like a sannyasin left out in the cold.

And to this day, I don't know anything about relationship! So you, my friend, are on your own. I still don't know anything about relationship except I have learned the hard way that relationship is a verb called relating. But I did, as you know, found the Geetam Sannyas Ashram in Lucerne Valley, California, for Osho in '75, which turned out to be the biggest meditation center in the States, and my now ex-girlfriend never stepped onto the property once. It goes to show you never can tell. Meditation, like love, is not what you think.

I never saw my ex again but I did have the good fortune of meeting the Buddha along the way.

While Christians all over the civilized world are upset that Jesus died on the cross, Buddhists all over the East are meditating on Buddha's famous statement, "If you meet me on the road, kill me." What Buddha meant is if you meet me in meditation you're dreaming about me, so in order to wake up, you need to destroy your dreams. Closer to home, when you meet your father in your mind, you may well feel a need to chop his head off. This thought may well bring guilt to the rescue. And thus a vicious circle is created that often leads to the leading health care in the West

173

relaxing into yourself." Osho

today, Prozac and her first cousins. Ah the marvels of Western medicine. Medicine and meditation come from the same root word; medicine is for the body and meditation is for the soul. Both words start with "me," so choose your "me" accordingly. By the way, I'm not suggesting that you physically kill your parents before you go to sleep tonight, and using this book as your defense when you plead insanity in a court of law. What I am saying is that in order to be alone you need to ask all of the judges that live inside of you to take a hike. I include in these inner judges not only the bad guys, like your parents and your first-grade teacher, but also the good guys, like Jesus and Buddha. Everybody has to go in order to find inner peace. So here is a question for you: If you get rid of the cowboys with the black hats as well as the cowboys in the white hats, who are you? If you are alone, do you as a personality actually exist? Now you may begin to understand when I say to you that when you are alone there is no one home. So when you are lonely, your mind is full. And when you are alone, you are in a state of no-mind. My words are simply an indication of the truth. As Osho would often say to me, "I am not the moon; I am a finger pointing towards the moon. Don't look at me, look at the moon." Simply inquire into your own life. And wake up.

I noticed that I often refer to parents and teachers and politicians as bad guys. This may not be true for you. They may, in fact, be saints, but be very alert, that it's easier to shoot a bad guy than to ask a saint to leave you alone. In all the group therapy I've ever participated in, the people who thought they'd had a delightful childhood and fabulous parents were the last ones to embrace aloneness. May I suggest Dynamic Meditation?

I am offering you a chance to kill the Buddha within because it may be easier for you to kill a Buddha within than a Christ. Most,

174

if not all my friends, dream about their very own God. The dream we live with during the day is the dream we have when we are asleep. Dreaming is dreaming is dreaming.

So I hereby give you complete permission to kill the Buddha in your dreams. Kill him because he is in your way for you to become yourself and the Buddha will die with a smile on his face because he knows that he was never there in the first place. It's your dream, not his. Enjoy yourself. And become a no-self while you're at it.

The idea of this book is really not about getting out of Buddha's way, it's about getting out of your own way. And I want to take this opportunity to thank everyone that has been in my way that I took seriously because it gave me a chance to look at my own life.

A meditation of the moment;
The Work of Byron Katie

Who would you be without your story Krishna Prem? My gosh, earlier in my book I mentioned I had gone beyond jealousy. Well much to my surprise when my beloved recently challenged me when she casually said she was beginning to leak. She said not one but many men were catching her fancy. I didn't freak out as much as you. Or maybe even less then you. I don't compare myself to others because comparison is hell. But, yes, it is time to look at jealousy one more time.

The Work is the baby of Byron Katie, and Katie puts it this way,

"I discovered that when I believed my thoughts, I suffered, but that when I didn't believe them, I didn't suffer, and that this is true for every human being. Freedom is as simple as that. I found that suffering is optional. I found a joy within me that has never

175

disappeared, not for a single moment. That joy is in everyone, always."

When I can't get out of my own way, I often bounce off my good friend Sagar who does The Work with me.

Sagar asked me four questions and what he calls a turnaround, which is a way of experiencing the opposite of what you believe. The questions Sagar asked me wer;e

1. Is it true?
2. Can you absolutely know that it's true?
3. How do you react when you believe that thought?
4. Who would you be without the thought?

The turnaround for me was realizing that my partner would much prefer to spend quality time with me.
When I first encountered these questions they seemed merely intellectual. The only way to understand how they function is to use them yourself.

Please consider looking into the work yourself www.thework.com.
Or you can bounce off Sagar at
www.changeyourmindchangeyourlife.org.

"Until you question what you believe, you remain the innocent cause of your own suffering."
Byron Katie

"Try not. Do or do not. There is no try." Yoda

Chapter 7

Tantra: The Supreme Understanding

"Love has nothing to do with somebody else, it is your state of being. Love is not a relationship. A relationship is possible, but love is not confined to it, it is beyond it, it is more than that. Man becomes mature the moment he starts loving rather than needing. He starts overflowing, he starts sharing, he starts giving, and when two mature persons are in love, one of the greatest paradoxes of life happens, one of the most beautiful phenomena... they are together, and yet tremendously alone; they are almost one. But their oneness does not destroy their individuality. How can you dominate the person you love?"

The True Sage, Osho

I like the word interlude. It comes from two Latin words; inter means between and ludus means games, so interlude means between games. So, why not for a few moments each day, just take off all the hats you're wearing and drop all the games you're playing and just be yourself, no hats, no games, just U.

You can't change the past but you can ruin a perfectly good present by worrying about the future. Some of us think we are the sum of everything we've done up to this moment in time, that we are our life history. For some of us, I guess that's quite comforting if we have a bright, shiny resume sparkling with glorious successes behind us, while for others of us it's rather disconcerting, if we have only a limp pile of lousy failures. But are we really that heroic act we performed ten years ago, or that DUI ticket we received last year? Does our past define who we are?

Well of course this reminds me of my own past. There was a time when I was trying to get away from myself, rather than look at myself or find myself, and I thought I could do it through drugs. So I fell in love with ecstasy, and I remember one particular time, around 1985, in California, when I was staying with a girlfriend. She was a pretty direct kind of girl, so one day she told me she was interested in having a sexy time with me and asked me if I would like to do ecstasy with her. Not surprisingly, she managed to convince me. So we went out, bought loads of bottles of water, and each took a pill.

Now I hadn't really done any drugs before, except for the occasional, casual inhaling of plant life to blow off steam and on the other end of the scale, swallowing diet pills so I could pull all-nighters in college cramming information into my mind. So being the enlightened soul that I was, I thought that this little pill wouldn't have much of an effect on me. Well, to say that it didn't make me ecstatic would be lying. My god, it was just beautiful! So there we were tripping on ecstasy, in this little place by the beach in California, and even though it was a bit chilly, I was paddling around in the water just laughing at the sky and feeling really open and free. It really was wonderful, and I have to say that on this particular occasion, the drug experience really was better than my day-to-day reality.

What a great name for this drug; ecstasy! My heart seemed to keep opening and opening like a flower, and I began to feel more and more loving, not to mention more and more sexy. And this girl who I kind of liked, suddenly by the end of an hour, I had fallen totally in love with her. Just holding hands with her I felt like I was melting into her. Just taking a pee in the sea felt like I was having an orgasm. Just sipping water felt like I was drinking liquid gold; wow, it was amazing! I laughed to myself at that old saying we had

"So just watch. Just get back a little and watch. Create a distance between you in the 60's, "Reality is for friends who can't handle drugs." Then, of course, we went home, massaged each other and made love; life was simply poetry and we had a magical day. And I felt maybe this was it; maybe I had found what I was looking for in this little tiny pill. But, as we all know, drugs don't last forever, so after four or five hours of gossiping, making love and drinking water, I soon fell back down to earth.

And that's the way it is with ecstasy. After this incredible euphoric high where you think you are in paradise with your dream lover, suddenly you find yourself plummeting down into the deepest depression ever. Then I guess you have to decide whether to do it all again, knowing big lows follow big highs, or whether to simply return to your life and sort things out there. You have to decide whether you want a substance to run your life, or whether you want to steer your own ship. So, what I discovered was that in the end, drugs don't solve anything. You can't run away forever from your own pain and suffering. Drugs weren't the doorway to higher consciousness, just a journey into the mind. They weren't the doorway to true bliss and lasting fulfillment; they just made me really excited and animated for a short time, then set me down again. Drugs didn't make me more me, and ultimately were an obstacle to me waking up.

And maybe, at this point, you're having some judgments about drugs or about me for having taken them, and that's OK, although, I will never be able to become the president of the United States. I feel good about these experiences and also about leaving them where they belong – in the past. And where is that past now? Gone, finished, died, never even happened. This brings me to the point that I am not the person who tried drugs all those years ago or the clean machine who no longer takes them. I am not my past

179

life or even lives, and you are not yours. I am fresh and new in each moment, and it's time to lighten things up;

It's a bright sunny day in the woods. A pink rabbit is happily running through the meadows towards the forest. Just on the edge of the wood, he sees a baby deer, smoking a joint, and stops to ask him, "What are you doing on such a bright sunny day like this? Drop your joint and come running with me in the woods!"

The baby deer drops his joint and starts running behind the rabbit, and as they run along, they reach a bench in the forest where a fox is sniffing cocaine.

The rabbit asks the fox, "What are you doing on a day like this? Can't you feel your heart? Can't you see the sun shining? Drop your cocaine and come run with us in the woods!"

The fox drops her cocaine, gets up, and starts running along behind the others, until they reach a darker part of the forest, where in a shady corner they find a wolf, shooting heroine. The rabbit happily bobs up to the wolf, "What are you doing on a day like this? Can't you hear the birds singing and nature celebrating? Drop your heroine and come run with us in the woods!"

The wolf slowly looks up and says, "My god, every time the rabbit takes ecstasy we all have to run with him in the woods!"

I remember Ram Dass and Be Here Now, and I remember that when he went to see his master Neem Karoli Baba for the very first time, it is said that he introduced Neem Karoli Baba to acid. And it did not change a thing for Neem Karoli Baba, he just went on and on about love and being yourself and being authentic and all the things our masters always try and get us to understand. And Ram Dass was very impressed that acid did not affect the consciousness

"Women who seek to be equal with men lack ambition." Marilyn Monroe

of his master and he went on to write the book Be Here Now which was, for many of us, the first introduction to meditation, along with the Beatles, along with the Maharishi Mahesh Yogi. This was the beginning of meditation as we began to hear about it in the West, at least for my generation.

Timothy Leary reminded me the one time we met in an all-night diner on route 1 in California, not to get married within seven days of taking ecstasy, because your heart just seems to open up; illusion, no illusion. Osho mentioned in discourse that the drug ecstasy was a lazy man's way to false enlightenment. That it gave friends a false experience of love. At least that is what I think I heard him say. And now I agree with him but at the time it felt great to me. I am glad I woke up to the truth after a good time was had by all. He said that taking it once was an excellent opener but not to take it more than that. For me it was a good experiment, and an indication to me to go deeper in love and awareness, and not to get confused between me and the experience. To be honest it was bigger than thought. You fall into the body and your heart opens.

I remember hearing that in a particular monastery in Thailand, young boys sent by their families in order to learn to meditate, to become monks, to serve mankind, and at the age of thirteen they are given magic mushrooms. Magic mushrooms are more of an organic form of ecstasy; you still have wonderful sensuous feelings, wonderful sensuous colors. And at the age of thirteen you have this experience, guided by the older monks. If at any time after age thirteen or after this experience of taking mushrooms you wanna take mushrooms again, you are welcome to do so but not as a monk. You have to leave the monastery. And for me it was always a wonderful guidance because I really, really liked this ecstasy, and if I felt that I needed to take it again I would have to leave meditation behind. Meditation is an organic form of life, ecstasy in all its glory is a chemical, a chemical reality. So I wish I could tell you that I only took ecstasy once and that I never needed to return, that I was so comfortable in my meditation that drugs were simply an altered state of reality which I could see for what it really is. But it's not the case. It was a wonderful time. I did ecstasy quite a bit over the next couple of years; I pretty much dropped meditation and preferred to just take life as a game in pill form. I had a lot of good times, I threw a lot of good parties, I had a lot of ups followed a few days later by a lot of downs.

It's not easy for me to speak of the time when I was in love with ecstasy, the time when I was just trying to get away from myself through drugs, the time when meditation was certainly not what I would be writing a book about. I know a lot of you probably hate me just knowing that I am not perfect. I think what we have to look at is not what a person did, but what he is doing right now. I am finished completely with drugs and I feel really good about the experiences I have had and I feel really good about leaving it in the past. So for a moment take a look at whether you can continue reading this book without judging me for what happened. It has always been a problem for me that alcohol is legal and that marijuana and ecstasy, which I consider soft drugs, are illegal. And that so many people are having a drink right now and judging a person who is lighting a marijuana cigarette up. I think it's just the way we have been told to behave. So let's just say again that you are not the drugs that you take but that the drugs that you take can be addictive. Are you controlled by a substance or are you free? And it's different for everyone. I personally do not like the feeling of being addicted to anything at all. I like to think that everything is something to try on and take off, that it's not my boss. I feel very deeply for people that are addicted to drugs. I feel like drugs have their own personality and they can often overwhelm us if we don't

"It is not the load that breaks you down, it is the way you carry it." Lena Horne

feel good about ourselves. I know after a cup of coffee how much more energy I have to share a thought. And it's cute, even coffee has its own personality. Herb tea has its own personality. It's a question of how much does this affect your personality and would you ever be able to see that you are not your personality if you are addicted to drugs of any kind, from caffeine to nicotine to ecstasy and beyond. That chapter in my life is now closed, and I would also like you to be looking at life straight ahead instead of through rose-colored glasses.

It's over twenty years now since I took ecstasy but it had an effect on my life. Maybe because it was a big experience and it felt good and it was hard for me to judge people taking it and it was hard for me to let it go and to be myself again, to just rest in myself instead of resting in the high of a drug. It was not something that I really looked at, and I almost find it difficult even to share with you. I guess I am probably still in judgment myself.

One other thing that happened for me that was so interesting is just to share I was in Goa on a vacation with my girlfriend, Jwala, and Goa is pretty famous for parties and you should be very aware of the punch that you are drinking. And I was at a party and a very good friend of mine came by with a punch and in my naivety I put the punch to my lips and I knew right away that it was MDMA or ecstasy because I had had a lot of experience. And I have never, in the ten years that I had been with my friend Jwala, ever taken drugs and she certainly wouldn't take ecstasy. So I told her that I took some by accident and it was very nice because when we went home that night, what I did is I told her I was really ripped and really stoned and I was basically faking it. And when we made love that night I was faking that I was stoned and she was quite enjoying the fact that I was so inanimate with her. You know after ten years you are little bored with each other and so I literally did

183

what you see women do so many times in movies, I faked that I was on ecstasy. I just had so much fun that the fun actually captured me and I had a great time and Jwala had a great time and I did not take drugs at all and that's fun.

I always like the little boy who goes to his father and he says to his father, "If I don't smoke, drink, take drugs or fuck, will I live longer?" and his father thinks about it and says, "Well, I don't know but I think it will seem longer."

Maybe what I am trying to point out here is that when Osho did come to America and he stole my thunder, I broke up with him so to speak. I took a break; I went into my own life. I went out of love and I went into drugs. And now I wanna speak about coming out of drugs and going into awareness. In the beginning of course I was just stumbling all over myself. I am just not that kind of guy. I don't think my teacher has ever been awareness and that does not mean that you do not need awareness, or that you can't even learn from awareness when you are not aware. It's always easy to be strong and invulnerable. Maybe like your dad. And it's easy to be weak and vulnerable. Maybe you think that is a female quality, but the trick is to be strong and vulnerable.

Just a joke I remember that I first heard in Amsterdam that really made sense: In Amsterdam in the very center of town is the Vondel Park and Doctor Watson and Sherlock Holmes were camping out one night in the park. And they had had some really great dope from the Bulldog Café. They nodded off around midnight and around three o'clock in the morning Sherlock Holmes woke up Doctor Watson and said to him, "Tell me what you see?" and Doctor Watson looked at his watch and he said, "I see it's around three o'clock, let me go back to sleep, let's talk in the morning." And Sherlock Holmes said, "No, this is important, I

"Don't confuse your personality with reality." Krishna Prem

need to know what you see." And Doctor Watson is aware that Sherlock Holmes is a master pain in the ass, that he means business and he won't let him go back to sleep until he comes up with a great answer. So he said, "I can see millions of stars in the sky. It's gonna be a beautiful, cloudless day tomorrow. Amsterdam at its best. I can see the universe expanding. I can even hear Jesus say, "God is love." I can hear Osho poking Jesus in the ribs with his elbow saying, "There is no such thing as god." How does that sound? Can we talk more in the morning over a cup of coffee?" and Sherlock Holmes says to Doctor Watson, "Doctor Watson for once in your life get real. Somebody stole the tent!"

So yes, maybe god is love. Maybe Osho is right when he says there is no god, and therefore how can god be love? But let me be clear that Osho says, "Love is my message. Let it be your message too." And let me clear that you need two legs to stand on, one leg is love and one leg is awareness. Without standing on both your legs, running your life is totally exhausting.

Recently I was asked by my friend and professional runner, Henry Dullink of run2day magazine, (www.run2day.nl) "Is running a meditation?"
Here's some of what I wrote;

"Yes… in fact if you can run, then there is no need for any other meditation – it is enough! Any action in which you can be total becomes meditation, and running is so beautiful that you can be totally lost in it. And you are in contact with all the elements – the sun, the air, the earth, the sky; you are in contact with existence. When you are running, your breathing naturally goes very deep and it starts massaging the hara centre… which is in fact the centre from where meditative energy is released. It is just below the navel, two inches below the navel. When breathing goes deep, it massages that centre and makes it alive."

185

This is a quote from Osho, whose favorite meditation as a young man was running.

And I went on to repeat what I said earlier in the book that many athletes talk about being in the zone. What they're referring to is doing an activity until they realize that they are no longer doing it, and it is happening by itself. Many marathon runners have reported that somehow after running and running for miles, they then get into a zone where they almost literally just sit back, relax and watch the running happening. This happened to me when I was in the U.S. Army Reserves, as I already told you, and the experience never left me. When I was discharged from the Army I found myself on my way to India to look more deeply into the zone as you might call it. I wanted to give peace a chance. In India, I met my friend and teacher and fellow runner, Osho.

Meditators, as well as runners, experience the same thing; they get into a space where they start to see themselves doing things, yet feel they are not doing it. They are even watching themselves meditating. So, if we are somehow able to sit back and watch what the body is doing, then who are we and who is doing the doing? In spiritual circles, people boldly say, "You are not the doer!" But if you are not the doer, then who is? If you are not making it happen, then who is?

In the small picture, our little local life as runners, we're doing, while in the big picture as godmen we're just being! Life is not only about enjoying what you do; it's about enjoying who you're being too. Period.

So yes, maybe God is love. Maybe Osho is right when he says there is no God, and so how can God be love? But in fact, it's about being aware of love. It takes both legs; the leg of love and the leg of awareness walking together in order to get centered, in order to be here and now, in order for your body to be walking and you sitting inside of yourself.

"Love is not a passion, love is not an emotion. Love is a very deep

I am not the kind of guy that looks at cars; it's a little sloppy for me, I look at the bumper stickers. People pass me by when I ride my bicycle and I see what is hanging out on their car, to see if there is any movement in the west towards enlightenment, towards non-attachment, towards humor. And one of the bumper stickers I saw the last time I was in town was "It's never too late to have a happy childhood." Whoever came up with that is on to something.

One of the things that helped me the most is something that Osho said to me or at least I heard him say – I never know because when I hear something that Osho said even to you, if it rings true for me, he said it to me directly. And funnily enough if he says something that doesn't ring true for me, I may meditate on it until it is mine. That's called trust or love for someone that you respect. Anyway what Osho said is, "When you go back into your childhood, when you go back into your memory, when you use hypnosis to go back and see what happened for you in this lifetime, do me a favor; don't relive that moment, live it for the very first time." And what this means is that often when we go back into our childhood and we were being fucked over by a loving parent or our coach or absolutely by our priests that are politicians, we see that we had no defense. We did not know who we were and that we were being fed all that information. When you go there now as an adult, as a mature human being, when you go back into that situation, live it for the very first time. You might say, "My god, when I was a little boy I fell for that crap. But now I don't, I am gonna stand up for who I am. I might even still be wrong, but I am certainly not going to take it sitting down. I am certainly not going to live like a coward again. I am certainly not gonna respect people that I don't give a shit about or I was just too little to say 'what? Is that what is going on? Is that how you treat people?'" So live it for the very first time does not mean that you actually start punching

understanding that somebody somehow completes you." Osho

people in your hypnosis session. They meant well but maybe they were not looking into their own lives, they were just sharing bullshit with you. Often times when I go back and I feel in my childhood that I did not have the guts to be real or I did not have the wisdom to be real. I just take little Michael by the hand and I say, "I am grown up now little Michael, I am a big Michael now. I am gonna take you by the hand and we are gonna walk through the situation and we are gonna be ourselves. And let that guy talk to somebody else. Let that priest mention what he doesn't know and yet he is willing to tell you what he does know. Come on now, just take me by the hand and let's leave. Let's get out of the situation, let's grow up. Let's spend time with people that we respect and that we love. I wanna wake up with you and be a successful person."

I was just remembering something that Osho shared with me. It was a time when I was leaving India and I was going to California and you remember I said that he loved when I said I was going to California. And he said, "Well, tonight when I speak, I would like you to sit very close to me. I have a message for you." I got excited, a personal message for me in public in front of fifteen thousand people because this was a public event and when a master speaks in Mumbai, fifteen thousand people is actually a disappointingly small crowd. I got there early because I wanted to sit next to Osho and of course everybody else had had the same feeling. I wasn't sitting very close but to be honest with you, I never had that feeling that sitting close was anything important for me; some people like to sit on his lap; I did not have that feeling. I was already in love and I could see people really working hard to be close to him. It just never was a major concern. When I say I was leaving Osho, for me the poetry was in leaving him. Going to America at that time and sharing meditation with friends and speaking about Osho; that was my life. I really enjoyed myself.

"If you love somebody, let them go, for if they return, they were always yours.

Being near him I often slipped into unconsciousness, and I have also been conscious far away from him. So I never had that problem. I many times sat with him and to be honest where I really got stoned was through just sharing. I guess that's one of the reasons I am writing this book. Anyway, that night can you believe it; fifteen thousand people and Osho was going to give me a personal message. I was pretty excited and the talk, believe it or not, was in Hindi. He might have been giving me a personal message all night long, but I don't speak Hindi and I just sat there and said to myself, "Shit." Right in the middle of this one and half hour Hindi discourse and you can imagine, I think in America we'd call it a snorer, I basically was nodding off, passing out, sitting on the ground, uncomfortable as hell, what am I doing here, this is foolish…and then in the middle of the one and half hour lecture, discourse, darshan, whatever you wanna call it he said, "Do not build a house on the bridge." And he said this in English; do not build your house on a bridge. And it was incredible. It was like a search that began that moment. I just kept repeating that sentence to myself for years. What the hell does that mean? "Do not build a house on the bridge." And it has been really beautiful for me.

Sometimes we call this a Zen koan, and I wanna tell you what I came up with, it may be wrong, and you might come up with something better and more enlightened. But basically we are just taking a walk this lifetime and we are looking into our own lives and many times you have heard the expression "the journey is the goal," and that's also a Zen koan, but basically most of us are not satisfied until we reach the goal and there is no goal so how are you going to reach it? Again I would like to use that expression "the seeker is the sought." A whole lifetime we are walking over this bridge, we are seeking and who we are seeking is who we

189

already are. So what I got from meditation on "do not build the house on the bridge" was never stop, be a rolling stone. Never accumulate, never own, live in a house but don't let the house own you. Drive a car but don't let the car own you. Yes, have material things but don't let the material things possess you. So often when we keep up with the Jones's or when we keep up with Krishna Prem or whoever we are keeping up with, we end up being owned by our own material objects. So I really got it. Osho wanted me to keep on moving, he always used to say to me, "God is movement." So I am continually walking across the bridge in search of myself and he said don't stop and build a house on the bridge. Don't stop and forget that you are in search. Even though you are in search of no-self, even though the seeker is the sought, I have never met anyone who knew this without knowing it. So until you know it, the engines are turning, you are in movement, you are crossing the bridge and Osho said, "Don't stop, do not build the prison called home. Just be in movement until one day the seeker disappears into the sought. The journey disappears into the goal. The goal disappears into the journey and the sought disappears into the seeker. You become a not-you. You become authentic unto yourself. The witness is born; the witness makes you a Buddha." This witness is the whole essence of what I am trying to share with you during the course of this book; this witness that can see but cannot be seen.

Another bumper sticker I saw said, "Do not Judge." Signed by J.C. Isn't that all we really know how to do? I have never met a Christian that wasn't an expert at judging me for not being a Christian. And did you ever meet a Jewish person that did not judge a Christian? I mean judging is what we do best because we have been told not to do it. Ok, so try this; just for fun I am going to suggest to you not to think of a really exciting member of the

What did the Buddhist say to the hot-dog vendor?"Make me one with everything."

opposite sex while you read the next five pages. For the next five pages I don't want you to think of anybody that excited you more than the written word. Take a moment now, and just picture someone that you would love to have dinner with, or spend the night with. Just imagine that person; don't tell anybody who you are thinking about right now. This is just between you and yourself. Now take a moment, put this book down. And don't think about this person.

If you were able to do this I am wrong and congratulations.I know I have already thought of the person I was not thinking about! Ok, so maybe what Jesus meant when he said do not judge, he was talking as much about not judging ourselves for doing it. You don't know who that person is, you may not know what he does, you may be empowered to put him in jail, you may be empowered to hurt him in some way, but that doesn't mean you know who that person is. You don't know where he is coming from; your head is not on his shoulders.

But I don't really know. I still don't know and even when I remember this story I kind of lose my center and even though I am saying be the witness, in moments like this the witness disappears and the anger appears. I say this chuckling but you know what I am saying. I can say that I am not my body but if you punch me on the nose because you did not like my book, I am probably gonna be my nose for a while until I shake it off. The witness is usually happier when he is healthy, so if you punch me on the nose I may lose a beat. What can I say?

It does look like I am one of those love guys; I love Osho and therefore I became enlightened. I love the master and therefore I became love. But that was part of my training. I do wanna say it's like one leg is love and yes, I learned a lot by hopping around on

191

one leg. I was exhausted; you cannot just be love without becoming exhausted. Whenever you are out of balance, even when you are just love, you are gonna get tired. If I call your left leg love and you just jump up and down on your left leg all day long, sooner or later you are gonna be out of balance, you are going to get tired, you are going to fall down. Because there are two legs in meditation; the first leg is love and the second leg is awareness. And for me I began with love because to be honest, that's what I needed to do. I needed love in my life and I was really willing to go bananas to have that experience. How did I know this? Well, often times of course you know after the fact and I think I can explain it really, really simply. You can probably see by now I have been coming and going to India quite a few times and I had started Geetam, which meant that my work was in California and then when I visited Osho in Pune, India, I would only visit for three months at a time and it was very clear that I was to be in Pune to enjoy myself. To work somewhat, but not to be confused because my work nine months a year would be at Geetam Rajneesh Sannyas Ashram in Lucerne Valley, California.

And then one day it happened. Osho came to America. Now this was a very interesting moment for me because in a certain way I was Osho in America. I was running a leading center and by now it was very, very popular; not only were people visiting, but people were buying books, buying tapes, and writing to us. I was in charge of that correspondence, and of selling the tapes and books and I was having a lot of fun. I can't begin to tell you, it was great. I certainly got over the fact that Krishna Priya never came to Geetam. I loved being single and I had some great moments. I don't know what to say, but it certainly was fun being Osho in America. And when Osho showed up it was like my god, I was no longer poetry, I was no longer suggesting that I knew Osho and

"There is nothing permanent except change." Heraclitus

you didn't and you better get on the next plane; I was effective and I meant it. I really did think you would benefit by going to India and you know what a good salesman I can be; I love my own product and there was no product at all. So many, many, many people went to India with my guidance and many people benefited from it. But when Osho came to America in 1981 my cover was blown, my work was over.

And in some ways that was the end of my love story. It's not that I did not love Osho anymore, but I just chose not to participate while he was in the States. I did not have the job anymore, Geetam became Osho's, the whole university that Osho was running in Pune, India, came directly and took over Geetam. Instead of running Geetam, I became a dishwasher. And funnily enough I kind of like washing dishes but it was a hit, and I think you can maybe understand if you were the president of the bank and now you are the janitor of the same bank, it may be difficult on your fucking ego guy. I know it was difficult on mine. Even though in meditation we are here to destroy the ego and I totally agree that enlightenment is the destruction of the ego, it still hurt. It's like my ego got a pop on its nose.

I began my journey on my other leg, which is called awareness. Now before I get into that I imagine that a lot of you are probably saying at this point in the book, "Krishna Prem is going to tell us why Osho had ninety-three Rolls Royce's, why Osho had one hundred and twenty-five square miles in Oregon to manage and what was he doing in America?" And to be honest, it's not anything I know about. I just wish I could tell you everything but your guess is as good as mine, because as soon as he came to the States, I just dropped out for a while. I was still Krishna Prem and I still visited the ranch for annual celebrations, in fact I went to four celebrations in a year, but I was in the world at that time being a bodyworker. I was basically out to pasture. And I guess Osho just liked Rolls Royce's. I don't know, it has never been important to me. He had ninety-three Rolls Royce's and I had one red Beetle convertible. I would love to tell you that story because that's kind of a love story too;

So Osho had ninety-three Rolls Royce's and I was about to be gifted one very cute, one of those red Beetle convertibles from Germany, cute, cute, cute, cute, cute. I left Geetam with just my orange clothes and backpack and nothing else, not a penny. And off I went to Venice, California. I was totally courageous and if I had any awareness at all, I probably would have been scared, but this was the beginning of jumping on that leg called awareness.

There I am in Venice, California and the place is filthy. I just can't see anything clean. All that stuff called cleanliness is close to godliness; I don't know, there is something in it. I don't know what it is by the way, you can tell me when you find out, but basically Venice Beach was filthy, and I started to look around to find something clean and nice. I finally found a Volkswagen camper van and it was spotless. And when my eyes went down to the bumper, there was a picture of Osho on a very, very famous bumper sticker and it read, "Jesus saves, Moses invests, Bhagwan spends." It was a really, really funny bumper sticker and I couldn't stop laughing, and I was actually laughing out loud when the man on the third floor looked out his window and saw me, he said, "Krishna, stay right there." He came downstairs and he said, "I always wanted to thank you because when I met you at Geetam, you gave me my mala and introduced me to Osho." A mala is a string of 108 beads with a little picture of Osho at the bottom. Anyway then he said, "God, and I have never been able to repay you. Is there anything I can do for you?" And I said, "Well, I just popped into town and I don't have a place to stay and I don't have

194

meal to eat." He said, "I am just about to go out of town and I paid rent for the month, the place is yours." He also gave me 500 dollars and he bought me dinner. So there I am now with a place to stay, 500 bucks in my pocket and dinner. And we are just relaxing and another friend of ours comes over and he is a bodywork teacher. He is going to do a ten-week bodywork course and in those ten weeks you learn to do this form of deep-tissue massage. I asked how much the course costs because I needed a handle, I needed something to do. And it costs 500 hundred dollars. So I just turned around and gave him the 500 dollars and started the course the very next day, again with no money in my pocket. But with a place to stay, and there were odds and ends in the fridge that would keep me going for a few days.

As you can probably tell by now, I am hustler. The course was ten days over ten weeks and then you are supposed to practice during the week. So that's what I did. I took the first day of the course and then in between that and the next day, I practiced on people and I charged them ten dollars, which was very reasonable for what they call rebalancing massage. And I was good; I was good because I am not afraid to touch another human being. I love being with someone and I love touching them. What I was experiencing is that people wanted to talk to me about Osho still, but they did not wanna pay to talk to me. But if I talk to them during the session, they felt really good about giving me those ten dollars. And I had a successful little practice. I was doing really good, people brought their friends, I was doing great. I paid rent. I had rented a table, now I bought a table. I am actually doing really, really good, still in the moment, absolutely not ahead of this lifetime financially but really, really having fun. Then this beautiful Mexican girl named Bianca came to me for a session and as soon as I touched her, she just began to cry. And it turns out that her husband had committed suicide and I did not really know what to do with that, but just be loving, and give her a deep massage without hurting her, and at the same time she could get in touch with her feelings. And we basically very much enjoyed each other and she was very generous and we had a lot of fun. Not long after our massage work was completed, our relationship became more intimate, more beautiful and we were out driving in her Volkswagen convertible, the red one, and she was saying the difficulty for her is that she never ever got to say goodbye to him. She never had closure in her relationship and just at that moment an ambulance with a siren on passed us. It was only a Volkswagen, but of course this is in LA, so even the ambulance can't go very fast and I just did a u-turn, and I was tale-gating that ambulance and beeping the horn and saying to her, "That's your husband in the back of the ambulance. He is about to die, you need to say goodbye to him right now." I mean this girl burst into the tears and just started speaking to the back of that ambulance and crying her heart out and saying how much she loved him and how difficult it was for her but how much she could understand that this life was too difficult for him to be in. It was really, really beautiful, such a beautiful goodbye.

Now we have a police car following us because I am tail-gating the ambulance and I think we are on our way to, I think it was called Daniel Freeman Hospital in Marina del Rey, and the ambulance pulls in, my red Volkswagen pulls in, the police pull in. I say to her, "You know, I don't even have a driver's license, you better make this look very real or I am I going to get arrested." She jumps out of the car, she starts pounding on the back door of the ambulance, the police come up to me so I said, "Thank heaven you're here, we have to help this women. Please come and help
196

us." At that the police just got back in their car and drove off. They did not want anything to do with this woman and I don't blame them. And I saw it happening and I tried to drag her away from the back of that ambulance and I said, "It's fine now, the police have left. You can stop crying." But she didn't, she just kept on pounding the back of that ambulance. Finally the ambulance driver gets out of the cab, and he's also Mexican, and he is more concerned for her than for the guy in the back of the ambulance. We just sat her down on the sidewalk and she is crying in my arms and I thank the guy and I say, "Sorry about this, her husband just died and we are saying goodbye to him." It's almost like he got it. Finally he opened up the ambulance and it was a poor little boy that had broken his arm. He was more in shock from the girl hitting the back of the ambulance than from his arm being broken. The kid took his skateboard under his good arm and he tried to get on the skateboard with his bad arm and the driver just grabbed him and brought him inside and put him in the wheelchair. He did not need it but that's what they do I guess.

Anyway she was really howling by now, but finally she gets control of herself and basically the end of the story is she goes to live in Rajneeshpuram. Her last gesture was to throw the keys in my direction and say, "I guess I won't need a Volkswagen convertible at the ranch. There are no roads there yet. Enjoy yourself." And she just signed over the paperwork. Bianca gave me the car. So there I am now with my VW convertible, rent paid, got a massage table, life is pretty good, I am hopping around now on one leg called awareness. It will be a long time before I get exhausted again. So I have compassion for you, I have compassion for me now. It's not so easy being yourself on this planet earth, suburb of the universe.

we call it the present." KenSu

Stop for a moment, look and see who you are – right now. See who you are in that split-second gap between your thoughts, before your mind starts filling up with ideas. Maybe you don't know. Maybe you disappeared. It's only in those moments when our thinking stops, like when we experience shock or surprise, that we can actually glimpse our original face. It's only when we have no thoughts, memories or dreams, no concept of being a body or a mind, and no identity to hold on to, that we can come to know who we are, totally alive, fresh and new.

Another idea we have, is that we're the whole kit and caboodle, that we're our whole "personality." In other words, we're our name, age, gender, looks, sexuality, our education, qualifications, talents, family, and religion, nationality, past and future collectively. We're everything this human body-mind does, feels, thinks and says. So just for fun, let's build a personality, and to make it easy, let's do me. Ok, so we begin with one baby, fresh out the womb, day one on planet earth. We then give him a name and some basic details: Michael Mogul, born in Boston, 1943, American, male. We then add to that some childhood stuff like; raised by his sister, brought up Jewish, wanted to play for the Boston Red Socks. Mix in some teenage stuff; hated school, graduated anyway, wanted to be a lawyer, got a BSc. Now, let's throw in some adult stories; discharged from the army, worked as a bartender in London, lived thirty years in India, Together with some slices of the past; traveled round the world, meditated, and some slices from the future; may get a job, get married and have kids when he's eighty. Now, we blend in a few opinions from others; he's funny, crazy and cute. Sprinkle on some interesting facts; loves mango chutney, is allergic to work, and garnish with some miscellaneous details; Virgo with Taurus rising, partial to lobster, plays tennis. Voila! One personality coming right up.

"I choose to come from a position of love and create relationships the way I

You can try this at home yourself if you like. Anyone can do it, and in fact, everyone does it, and that's the problem. From the day we are born, we begin building this personality, this character, this story of me. And as the years roll by, so we keep refining it, reinforcing it and adding new lines to it. And we trot off to parties and share our story with others, and others share their stories with us. Oh, and of course, we discuss other people's stories too, "Oh, you know John, he's really sweet one minute and then a total asshole the next," and "You know that girl Cindy, she's not as shy as she looks." Then as soon as we have a few details down, we think we know who they are and we put them in a pigeon-hole. "Hmm, she's a Scorpio, must be sexy." "Oh steer clear of him, he's a Leo!" Oh no, cardboard cutout, or oh no, huge personality.

The word "personality" comes from the Greek word persona, which basically means a mask. Basically, we wear this personality like a mask, over the top of who we are. Generally we spend the first part of our life building our persona, developing our character and shaping our social mask. It's no coincidence that when we go through a rocky patch that others say, "Never mind, it's character-building." We can also mold it to look any way we like; we can put it on and take it off, and create both a public and private persona. First we need to create this personality and explore what it really is, before we can begin the process of dismantling it. That's what the journey home is all about, ripping off our social wallpaper and tearing down the walls of our identity, until we are standing absolutely butt-naked.

Basically, when we boil it all down, our personality is only a collection of information or data, thoughts about who we are, often expressed in words. But it's not solid, substantial or set-in-stone. In

would like to be treated. My need is to love." Veeresh

fact, it's amazingly flimsy and fragile, and can disappear at any moment. Our personality is who we think we are, and the key word here is think. We need to think to have a personality, and when we don't think, our personality doesn't exist. Have you ever noticed in moments when the mind stops, when we are in orgasm, shock or meditation, how we immediately lose our personality and become an empty slate? That is what this book is really about; it's about stripping away the layers of this personality to reveal our original face beneath.

Well, we've talked about personality and identity, I and me, but what about this other thing – ego? Typically, we use it to mean just plain arrogant, or when we want to say, "He's a bit full of himself," we might say, "He's got an ego the size of Texas!" Generally, we talk about it as if it's some nasty disease that some of us have and some of us haven't. But hair-splitting aside, it's just another word for our personality or identity, our idea of "I" or "me." Basically, we've all got the disease and we all suffer from it.

We talk about this ego as if it's a solid, substantial thing, when in truth it's nothing more than a collection of thoughts about who we are, floating through our minds. So when we read about killing the ego or going beyond the ego, it simply means dropping that story of who we are. Until we can clear the mind of all thoughts, we can't really see what is true. It's easy, it's simple, and it's not rocket science.

We probably spend the first part of our life puffing up this ego and strutting our stuff, yet only when our ego bubble bursts, can we see the reality; that it was only hot air. Then we can laugh at this crazy idea of me. Then we see no ego, feel no ego, be no ego. If you're experiencing your ego right now, then I can almost bet

200

you are your mind, you are indentified with your mind instead of being an individual with a mind.

Our personality or identity is simply a collection of ideas to be transcended. One way of looking at this is to imagine our whole personality as a house and each aspect of our personality as a window. As we have many aspects to our personality, so we have many windows in our house. And since we're always trying to improve our personality, we keep polishing the windows to make them cleaner and shinier. And because we tend to specialize in life, we tend to polish maybe one or two windows more than the others. Say you are a nurse, and then everyday you polish that window called nurse, because you think that window called nurse is you. And say, I'm living in the house next door to you and I'm a great meditator, then everyday I'll polish that window called great meditator, because I think that window is me.

So there we are, all busy polishing these little panes of glass, when all we need to do, is to just open the window and fly out. Then we will see that we are not the tiny window, not the whole house, but we are the limitless sky. Then, if we look down, we will see all those billions of people still stuck in their houses, polishing their windows, still thinking they're their personality. And if you laugh to yourself, "Hey now I'm free, but they're still stuck in prison," then there's a pretty good chance you'll just crash and burn. If instead you look down, and look really carefully, you'll see that everyone is doing the best they can, is going at their own speed, and is exactly where they're meant to be.

In the East they say there are many windows in a house but only one sky. There are many facets to our personality but only one U. And the great thing is that once you know you are the sky, then you can really have fun. You can go back into the house and make

201

can go." T. S. Eliot

all the windows shine, you can play at anything you want, because now you know you are already the sky. So you see, it's that simple, your house is not your home, and your personality is not your reality.

Well, by now you may be thinking... and why does it matter anyway, if I know who I am or not? And I would say in one sense, it doesn't matter at all. You are you whether you know it or not. You may be a sleeping you rather than an awakened you, and essentially life moves through you no matter what. Existence doesn't count on you to breathe, doesn't depend on you as a character in the play to wake up. Existence always is, regardless of what you do, say, think or feel. You are already free. So, if you don't want to wake up, great. If you're too busy living life, or don't really care, then no problem; just live, love and laugh and put this book down now.

And if you want to wake up and smell the coffee, also great! If you have that thirst to know, that urge to search and you do care, then it does matter. Just know that if you really want to awaken, you'll find your way and everything you need will become available to you. So if the possibility is there and you can wake up, then why not? Why do dogs lick their balls? Because they can!

But what can I say? I've been on both sides of the fence, and knowing who I am is beyond great. Being awake is infinitely and indescribably better than not being awake, and unfortunately, words will never be able to do it justice. Paradoxically, being awake doesn't mean everything's perfect, it just means you see no imperfections. It doesn't mean you get anything, it just means you know what already is. It doesn't mean you don't have bad days, it just means you enjoy all experiences. It doesn't mean you become special, it just means you are the most ordinary of all.

"Wisdom tells me I am nothing. Love tells me I am everything. Between the

I remember announcing to a hip sales gal at Starbucks that I am now enlightened. "How cool," she said, "...and that will be two dollars ninety-four for your latte." Basically, enlightenment doesn't pay the rent, hell; you don't even get your coffee for free.

Here's a joke for all you thirsty fish in the ocean of life;

I read once, that the way to achieve true fulfillment is to finish all the things you have started. So I went around the house and found all the things I had started but hadn't finished. Before leaving this morning, I polished off a bottle of red wine, a bottle of white wine, a coupla' glasses each of Bailey's and Kahlua and shot of Wild Turkey, a handful of Prozac and a few Valium, half a cheesecake and a box of chocolates.

You have no idea how freakin' good I feel!

You know, if we're not thinking we're our past, we're probably thinking we're our future. For most of my life I lived for the future. I always thought things were going to get better for me...tomorrow. I don't know when this whole idea started; it must have been when I was a kid. I remember thinking, "School sucks and I can't wait till I'm grown-up." Then when I graduated from school and got a job, I remember thinking, "Wow, work sucks; it's pretty tough out here in the world." Anyway, I did the best I could, and the funny thing was, I never really got too down in the dumps, because I always thought life was going to get better someday. Even when I met Osho, in India, I was still living in the future, and thinking "Maybe one day, I'll be able to sit beside him". And even though he was always going on about being here now, and not living in the future, I somehow at the time, just didn't get it.

So I know how it goes and I know why we do it. We're taught to plan ahead, save for that rainy day, and live for that bright, rosy

two, my life flows." Nisargadatta

future ahead of us, because today doesn't look so great. Or we're thinking "Maybe I'm not much now, but just wait a few years and then I'm gonna show everyone. Then I'm gonna really set the world on fire!" So sometimes we base our identity on who we're gonna be or wanna be tomorrow, because somehow we're not quite enough today. "Yeah, just you wait, you'll see, once I get that car, you won't be laughing at me then."

And you know, I'm not giving anyone a hard time for trying to achieve something or create a better life for themselves. I think it's great that many gasmen do become PhD.'s and directors. No, I'm not saying that at all. If you want to be a doctor, be a doctor, if you want to be a surfer, be a surfer. We all have to make our living somehow and better to love what you do than hate it. Only don't mistake what you're gonna do or who you're gonna be, for who you already are. Don't keep telling yourself the story that you'll be someone when…because when you're standing in that place in the future, you'll be thinking the same thing. Meanwhile, all your ideas, expectations, projections, ambitions and goals, and your becoming, stop you from being who you are right now.

Any who knows? Suspend your disbelief for a second…maybe who you really are is so much more than who you're intending to be? Maybe you already are everything you want to be? The journey home is not about becoming someone, about building or creating an identity, it's about stopping trying and seeing that you are already it. The truth is, you're not who you were yesterday, and not who you are going to be tomorrow, you're not in transit, U are already U, always have been and always will be.

I asked my friend's daughter once, "What are you going to be when you grow up?" She replied, "I'm not going to grow-up!" Wise kid. She's already it.

204

When Osho left his body in 1990, I was relaxing in my room in the commune, when suddenly there was a knock on the door from my neighbor, Niten. He was beside himself with tears as he told me that he was going directly to Buddha Hall as Osho had just left his body. It was interesting to me that he had his one-year-old son in his arms as he told me about Osho's death. His son was beaming just as loudly as Niten was crying, because he was so happy to see me, the absurdity of the situation didn't pass me by. I had a strange feeling of delight also come over me remembering that Osho said, "Celebrate everything including death." Needless to say I was filled with sadness and joy at the same time. I just don't know how to explain those moments, and you will only understand if you've had one yourself. I proceeded to Buddha Hall at exactly seven o'clock, just as Osho came to his usual spot on the podium, only this time he was covered with flowers, and ready to be cremated. We spent the evening singing and dancing while Osho's body was burnt. I knew it was OK with him that he died, but I can't say the same for myself. He was a father-figure for me, and I was very attached to his physical presence. His death was a wake-up call. I went back to my room around four in the morning, poured myself a stiff Scotch, and packed my bags. As the sun rose I went to the breakfast canteen to say goodbye, and I was simply amazed at the joy with which the food was prepared by my friends, and there was such a mixture of joy and sadness which I'd never felt before. Every funeral I'd ever gone to was filled with food and misery, this one was simply alive. I told myself this celebration will not last forever, so I won't unpack my bags, but I won't leave town before the party ends. And that, in fact, is over twenty years ago. I've learned more about meditation and celebration since Osho left his body than I knew in all the years that I was with him while he was in his body. I call this maturity even if you may consider it just the opposite. It's anyone's guess. All I can say is that I will never

"Love yourself, respect yourself, be gentle with yourself." Osho

consider death to be the end of the game ever again, and I hereby invite you to sing and dance when you hear that I have left my body. And the beat goes on....

"All the world's a stage, and all the men and women merely players, they have their exits and their entrances."

Shakespeare

Just before Osho left his body, the commune had bought the property adjacent to 17, Koregaon Park, with the original intention of building a new auditorium for meditation. My feeling was to not build a new meditation hall, but to actually develop the property with a swimming pool, tennis courts and gymnasium. If I was going to stay in India, and in Pune, I wanted to have some fun. This idea was embraced by the commune's Inner Circle, a group of twenty-one friends that Osho had chosen to run the place after he left his body. Within moments of my suggestion I was presented plans for a swimming pool, to be built immediately. The pool in the plan was organic in shape so as not to have to cut down any trees to build it, and as I studied the plan I had an eerie feeling that this plan was not drawn up by an architect. Mirrored in the pool were small yellow flowers, and I slowly began to smile as I realized this organic drawing was the work of none other than Osho himself. Again I felt the synchronicity of the master-disciple relationship. Osho and I simply had the very same idea. The girl that was showing me this plan was Anando, Osho's secretary at the time he left his body.

When Anando showed me the plans, and when I understood they were actually drawings from Osho himself, I just looked into her eyes and we both knew that the Osho International Commune was about to become the OSHO International Meditation Resort. I

206

welcomed the change and threw in my total support. And thus I began working for Anando, even though I couldn't keep up with her. She would just look back at me and laughingly say, "Wake up." Until one day I asked her how she became such a tireless worker. She laughed and said, "This is nothing compared to when Osho was in his body, at least now I can sleep at night. When Osho was alive he would sometimes wake me up every hour on the hour from midnight till sunrise for a Diet Coke®. It got so bad that I actually put on my bravest smile and suggested to Osho that I had found something that will tickle his fancy. I showed him a picture of the newest Diet Coke® machine from America. He could take his favorite cup, put it down on a metal plate, press a button and ice would come out. A second button and the exact amount of Diet Coke® would come out without spilling a drop. I felt this was the perfect gift for his birthday, a present from me to him, and Osho smiled at me and said, "Anando, you don't understand, I love to push your buttons." Eventually Osho's doctors insisted that he never drink Diet Coke® ever again, and Anando finally got a good night's sleep. If you ever have a chance to meet Anando though, she is a woman of beauty, grace and, might I add, infinite energy. Look her up for yourself at www.lifetrainings.com

Once upon a time, there was a bunch of tiny frogs who arranged a running competition. The goal was to reach the top of a very high tower. A big crowd had gathered around the tower to see the race and cheer on the contestants.

The race began, and no one in the crowd really believed that any of the tiny frogs would reach the top of the tower.

They said things like, "Oh, way too difficult!"

"They will never make it to the top."

"Not a chance that they will succeed. The tower is too tall!"

207

"Mistakes are a fact of life. It is the response to error that counts." Nikki

The tiny frogs began collapsing. One by one, except for those with fresh momentum, who were climbing higher and higher.

The crowd continued to yell, "It is too difficult!!! None of you will make it!"

More tiny frogs got tired and gave up, but one continued higher and higher and higher....

This one would not give up!

At the end everyone else had given up climbing the tower. Except for the one tiny frog that, after a big effort, was the only one who reached the top.

Then all of the other tiny frogs naturally wanted to know how this one frog had managed it?

They asked him how he had found the strength to succeed and reach the goal.

It turned out...

That the winner was deaf!

Finally, you are OK with my name being Krishna Prem. And with my teacher in India whose name is Osho. So now that you are feeling comfortable with strange names, let me throw an ancient Hawaiian technique at you just for good measure... get ready... Ho'oponopono. The modern proponent of this technique is Dr. Hew Len. I am touched by Dr. Len's simple demeanor and ability to share love and clarity. Folklore has it that Dr. Hew Len was able to cure mental illness in inmates from an entire psychiatric wing of a maximum security prison in Hawaii... not by seeing convicted murderers and rapists alike in person but by simply seeing their personal records at his office. The prisoners were cured by Dr. Len as a result of good doctor clearing the data within himself.

"A man cannot be comfortable without his own approval." Mark Twain

The meditation is simple and alchemical. The process goes like this…

I'm sorry.
Please forgive me.
Thank you.
I love you.

By living this mantra you are clearing the data or memories in your mind. For example, if you are having a problem with, say, your financial situation, just say over and over to yourself, "I accept responsibility for having no money. There is something inside me causing this problem. I am sorry, I love you, please forgive me and thank you." This will help you clear whatever memories or feelings you have regarding money.

Ho'oponopono is a happening. Please get yourself to www.youtube.com and search for Dr. Hew Len. He will blow your mind into No-Mind. If not, I'm sorry. Please forgive me. Thank you. And I love you.

Ps. Dr. Hew Len is a hard man to find in person. I have asked my friend Pinky Leela to field any questions you may have about Ho'oponopono. That's Pinky Leela (pinky_sidhu@hotmail.com). Ho'oponopono is her passion.

"See no ego, feel no ego, be no ego." Krishna Prem